# OVERALLS

# &

# WISDOM

## A Memoir of Unconventional Life Lessons

## Alisha Erickson

*Book Cover Design by: Rimsha Anwar*
**www.fiverr.com/rimshaanwar4046**


**ISBN:** 979-8-9996039-1-3


**Library of Congress Control Number:** 2025915912




*Rise While Rooted Publishing*

# Disclaimer

*This book is a work of memoir and reflection, and while it is based on real-life events, some names have been changed to protect the privacy of individuals. The stories, lessons, and reflections shared within these pages are presented with the utmost respect for the people involved and are intended to honor the impact they had on my life and growth. While the events described are true to my experience, they are presented in a way that focuses on the lessons learned, not on the individuals themselves.*

# For Dad and Mom, "Boss and Ma'am"

Thank you for the lessons that didn't come wrapped in lectures or textbooks but in everyday moments and your unmistakable style of wisdom.

You modeled hard work without complaint and integrity without exception. We never needed Webster to understand humility, your life illustrated it at every turn. You showed us how to push through the hard stuff and still jump in the puddles when things got too serious. Most importantly, you taught us the elusive art of how to recharge ourselves without neglecting our responsibilities and commitment to others.

This book is a tribute to the life lessons you lived out loud, as unconventional as they may have been. May your influence echo through generations, both as a compass and an anchor for all those who follow.

# For Addison

*May the unconventional wisdom passed down by your grandparents, "Boss and Ma'am," become more than just stories you hear. May their lessons take root in you, guiding you as your moral compass and reminding you always of where you come from and who you are.*

*These truths are your living inheritance, woven into the very fabric of who you are. One day, when you're walking your own children through the beautiful, messy, meaningful journey of life, I pray these same lessons rise up in your voice, your choices, and the strength of your heart. May they keep all of us grounded in the roots that shaped us and the love that holds us together across time and generations.*

# Table of Contents

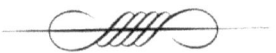

# Preface

Perhaps you've found yourself in a moment like this before, suddenly struck by the uniqueness of a situation you're a part of, overwhelmed by a deep sense of gratitude. It's the kind of moment where the images of your life flash through your mind, as if your memories have decided to parade past you in vivid color. That moment found me and it turned into more than a mural of memories. It became the spark that inspired me to write this book.

Growing up, I thought my family was like any other. The four of us were tight. My younger sister, Brittany, and I found a built-in best friend in each other, even though we were four years apart. Life struck a perfect balance between the silly and the serious, with my parents at the center, demonstrating what it meant to love deeply. They taught by example and life's most essential lessons were often tucked inside everyday moments and chores carried out. It didn't resemble a Norman Rockwell painting. It was quirky and unapologetically ours. It was beautiful.

As an adult, I realized just how unique and remarkable my upbringing had been. It wasn't rich in material wealth or even an abundance of books. It was rich in relationships and unconventional life lessons. My parents didn't hand out wisdom in tidy quotable phrases. Instead, they offered it in the form of lived experience, through moments that, at the time, seemed ordinary to me but, in hindsight, were actually quite extraordinary.

There was one pivotal moment in my adult life when I understood just how unconventional those lessons were and how deeply grateful I was for them. I realized that many of the values I carry- resilience, humility, the importance I place on relationships, and resourcefulness, had been passed down not through lectures or curriculum but through real, raw life. The kind that doesn't always make sense while you're living it but somehow fits together perfectly when you look back.

It was at that moment I knew I had to write this book, not as a how-to manual but as a collection of stories and reflections. Each lesson here was learned the long way and, in most cases, the unexpected way. My hope is that in sharing them, someone else might find clarity and encouragement or even just the comforting reminder that wisdom doesn't always come dressed in formal clothes. Sometimes, it arrives unannounced, barefoot, in overalls, strumming an air guitar.

# Introduction

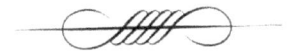

Growing up, Mom was the anchor of our family. She was predictable in the best way, the steady presence we all leaned on. She was our go to for everything and somehow she always kept the house immaculate, no matter how many muddy shoes or dirty dishes tried to get in the way. Hairspray, makeup, heels, and stockings were invariably part of her work regimen. She never hesitated to speak up if something bothered her. She was strong, sharp, and graceful, all at the same time.

Dad, on the other hand, brought with him a certain brand of chaos. Each evening when he got home from work, it was as if a tiny tornado had blown through the door. His "help" in the kitchen was always well-intentioned but inevitably led to a bigger cleanup job than if Mom had just handled dinner herself. There was still no denying his heart behind it and Mom recognized that.

His hands told the story of his work, thick, callused fingers, nails gnawed down to the quick, permanently stained black from old transmission fluid and grease. There was almost always some sort of fresh cut, mid-healing, as evidence of the latest project or fix-it job he was involved in. He didn't need to tell you what he did for a living, you could see it all over him. He worked with his hands, and he worked hard. He could build anything, fix anything, and figure out things that would leave most people scratching their heads. You might have called him a "man's man" but if you spent any time with him at all, you would quickly come to realize he was the ultimate softie, a sentimental soul who would go out of his way to make sure my mom, my sister Brittany, and I were never upset with him.

Dad had a certain look on the weekends. It typically involved a pair of overalls but summertime is when his look really garnered the attention of those who didn't know him. Since we grew up in the South, our summers were hot and humid but in Dad's eyes, overalls were still the perfect attire, they just needed a little custom alteration. Style was never a concern for him, he saw absolutely nothing wrong with cutting the legs off his overalls to turn them into cutoff shorts. Wearing a shirt under the overalls was optional, in his eyes, given the southern heat. Shirtless and in his cutoff overalls Dad mowed the lawn every weekend, leaving behind a perfect striped pattern.

Brittany and I often rode in the trailer hitched to the back of the lawnmower, dragging our bare feet through the cool, freshly cut grass until the soles of our feet turned green. We would pile into his pickup truck to go fishing, work in the massive garden we planted as a family each spring, and, later in the summer, stack firewood in the woodpile while he chopped it. There was always something to do, and somehow, we always did it together.

Dad welcomed us into his projects, big or small. In the fall, we became the turnip green pickers. Well, I did. Brittany had a favorite phrase growing up: "I don't even know how." We still laugh about it and now it's become part of our family's shared language often used to bring levity to life's frustrating tasks. That simple phrase got her out of a lot of work over the years. Strangely, it never bothered me. Even though I hated turnip greens, I didn't mind picking them. I'd fill plastic grocery bags full, and Mom and Dad would cook them down all day. The rest of the family would devour them at dinner, everyone except me. I was always the picker, never the eater.

One spring it was decided we needed a space to store the fishing boat and lawn mower, because the garage was getting cramped. This became our grandest project of all. Dad and I spent most of our days that spring in the backyard erecting a two-bay barn with a metal roof. Every weekend that spring (and some weeknights too), Dad and I worked on the barn, measuring, sawing, hammering. It was our weekend fun. Maybe it didn't seem like fun to Dad but I remember the immense sense of pride and accomplishment in being part of something so significant. In the years that followed, the barn's metal roof even served a second purpose: it became the go-to tanning spot for my best friend, Jessica, and me, long before pool season began.

Of course, not all of Dad's projects were particularly useful or productive but we happily pitched in with those too. Especially when they were more fun than functional. Brittany even got in on those. You see, Dad had a serious love for fireworks, the loud obnoxious ones that rattled your windows and lasted way too long. He would stock up on them during the Fourth of July and save them for some unexpected, random day or night. Brittany and I were his loyal accomplices. We would help him attach long strings of fireworks to the top of poles or high on tree limbs. Then, we'd play our best game of "nonchalant" inside as we waited for Dad to light them off and rush into the house, pretending like we had no idea where all the noise was coming from. Of course, the neighbors, eventually, caught on to our firework shenanigans. We didn't care. That didn't stop us from continuing the firework fun at Dad's direction.

Behind all the noise, projects, and overalls, one thing was always crystal clear in our home: Mom and Dad were a united front. They were ALWAYS on the same team. Their loyalty to each other was unwavering, and the respect they had for each other was never up for debate. Dad never referred to Mom with tired clichés like "the ol' ball and chain" or his "old lady." No one dared. The love they shared was visible in a thousand little ways and the foundation it built shaped us more than we realized at the time.

There were countless lessons we learned watching them navigate life. Lessons about the merit in strong work ethic and immeasurable value of showing up for each other. Many of those lessons weren't conventional. Then again, neither was Dad.

While these stories stem from the lessons learned from Dad, they were undeniably made possible by the strong woman who stood behind and often in front of every scene whom I have the privilege of calling Mom. You'll see her wisdom in what she held together and what she gently let go. She gave us the space to stumble, even when every fiber of her being must have longed to step in and shield us. She gave Dad the room to teach in the way only he could. These are some of the unconventional lessons on life and love from the man in cutoff overalls.

**Dad—the man in cutoff overalls.**

# UNCONVENTIONAL LESSONS

# Be Present and Engaged

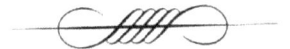

*"Hark I thought I heard a meadowlark, no that was only me I let a fart."*

Dad didn't learn to read until I was in kindergarten. Driven by the desire to read me a bedtime story, he set out to change his life with the help of my elementary school teachers. Learning to read wasn't just about acquiring a skill for him; it was about something much deeper. He wanted to be an engaged father.

His same commitment to presence and engagement showed up over and over in our lives. It's why he seized every opportunity to join my sister and me on school field trips. Though I was young, I will never forget the story he told my Mom after chaperoning one of my kindergarten trips. Another student, out of innocent curiosity, asked me a question that packed a powerful punch for my Dad:

*"Is that your real daddy?"*

He was my *real* Dad and he was the Dad who showed up, always present, always engaged. Looking back, it is clear that the words of a five-year-old that day revealed the true impact of his presence. What we loved, he loved. I came to realize it was a luxury not all children had.

As we grew older, his presence never wavered, he simply adapted, matching our interests step for step. He made it his mission to befriend all our boyfriends, never missing a chance to make our friends laugh or rally against him in the name of fun. He became the unexpected villain we didn't even realize we needed. While he played the villain, he was methodically becoming everyone's hero.

Take, for example, his unrelenting love for chaos disguised as comedy. When we were in middle school, he somehow got his hands on vials of the most disgusting pungent-smelling, stomach-churning spray imaginable. A single spritz would clear a room leaving everyone gagging and pointing fingers at each other. Without fail, we would find Dad doubled over somewhere, laughing so hard he couldn't breathe, tears streaming down his face as he watched the chaos unfold. Nothing delighted him more than watching people gag, clutch their faces in horror, and launch an all-out blame game of "Who did it?" All the while, he lurked in the corner, as the proud puppet master deeply satisfied his can of fart spray had cleared the room like a fire drill.

Moments like this were his sweet spot. He became the target of all our jokes and stories, exactly as he wanted it. He knew sometimes the best way to connect was to make himself the punchline. He was the guy who took pride in being the villain if it meant keeping everyone entertained. It was just one of his many unconventional ways of being a part of the party, the villain we all adored and could never get enough of.

*Dad, mid-growl, about to "attack" one of our friends.*
*One of his signature moves.*

He was a staple in the lives of our childhood friends, boyfriends, ex-boyfriends, and the families of those we spent time with. Our friends and their families often keep in touch with *him* more consistently than with my sister or me. Dad had this remarkable way of embedding himself into people's lives by showing up in unforgettable ways.

Whether through his slow, cupped handclap designed to stand out from the rest, a hidden squirt bottle of ice water to surprise unsuspecting victims, or his ridiculous duck walk meant to elicit embarrassment from Brittany and me and roaring laughter from all of our friends. Regardless of the tactic, you always knew when Dad was there. Of course, an audacious can of fart spray remained his ultimate calling card of our childhood, like his version of leaving a memorable autograph.

For all his antics, the real lesson was clear: being present was about showing up *fully*. Dad never let life happen in the background. He believed in being part of the action, the conversation, and ultimately the memories. He knew being engaged made all the difference.

The people who truly leave a mark are not always the loudest or the ones with the biggest titles. They are the ones who are present enough to make others feel seen and feel valued. They are the ones who will prank you and stand by you, even if it means becoming the unwitting villain in a fart-spray fiasco.

Dad showed us that being present was about proximity and connection. It is knowing when to be serious and when to squirt your kid's friend with ice water. It's about understanding that quality time together comes from showing up in the lives of the people you love because when you are truly present, you don't just make memories, you leave a legacy.

As unconventional as his methods may have been, he made others know they mattered by being present and engaged. Regardless of the role you are playing when you show up, be present.

# Follow Through on Your Word

*"Listen to your mother."*

As an elementary and middle school principal, part of my job is reassuring parents, many of whom are apologizing for something their child did at school, *parenting is the hardest job in the world*. It is, without question, the most rewarding but it is also the most challenging. It is like being the CEO of a chaotic, snack-fueled startup where your employees never listen and occasionally cry in the cereal aisle.

I was about eight years old when I first saw this truth play out in our home. It was Christmas morning. Brittany and I had finished opening our presents, leaving the living room, also the entryway to our home, completely littered with new toys. A clean house was a standard that could be upheld regardless of wealth and it was a value our Mom made sure we all embraced, regardless of whether we liked it or not. One thing was certain: our house was always spotless and Christmas morning was no exception.

The mess was allowed to stay for a little while but soon, it was time to put everything away. Our parents were social and the unexpected pop-in visitor on Christmas morning was almost a guarantee. Besides, we took pride in our home and in what we had. Mom had already cleared away the wrapping paper, bags, and boxes and Dad had taken the trash outside. That left Brittany and me to put away our new toys, once just hopeful circles in the Toys "R" Us catalog, now scattered across the living room floor.

Everything started off smoothly, until Brittany, my strong-willed, four-year-old sister (who, to this day, is my very best friend in the whole world), decided she was *not* going to pick up her brand-new baby doll. This was not just any doll; it was the *doll* of the year. The one that made grown adults sprint down department store aisles like Olympic athletes. The one everyone wanted. The one that was nearly impossible to find. The one people stood in Black Friday lines for hours just to get their hands on. The one our parents undoubtedly made personal sacrifices to buy. Yes, that one.

Mom kindly told Brittany to finish picking up her toys. A little while later, she followed up: "Brittany, *put your baby doll away.*" Both requests were ignored. On the third try, Mom's tone shifted: "Brittany, I *said go put your baby doll away.*"

Brittany's response? A bold, defiant: "No."

The entire time, Dad was in the kitchen, cooking. He had a remarkable ability to know what was going on without ever needing to interfere. Mom was undeniably the lead disciplinarian in our house, and he respected that. If she ever needed backup, she never had to ask, he just knew when it was time to step in and offer support, or to completely tap in so she could tap out and take a break (if you're a parent, or have ever tried reasoning with a stubborn four-year-old, you will understand the value of this role). It was just another way he protected Mom, always putting her first and supporting her in everything.

This was one of those moments.

Brittany was a child that never responded favorably to demands. I am convinced reverse psychology was discovered because of her and I was her sister not her mother. The more direct the demand the deeper she dug her heels.

*Brittany clomping around in Dad's boots in front of the wood-burning fireplace.*

Without raising his voice or leaving the kitchen, Dad spoke up: "*Brittany, if you don't pick up your baby doll like your mom said, I'm going to come over there and throw it in the fire.*"

Yep. He said that.

No, it was *not* pre-discussed with Mom.

He didn't storm over or shout, he simply stated, calmly, clearly, directly, what he was going to do to support her. In that moment, it was as if time stood still in our 1,300-square-foot home. There was an unspoken, unanimous prayer in the room: "PLEASE, *Brittany, just pick up your baby doll.*"

Did she? Nope.

The expectation was set and the threat was now made. In the corner of our living room sat a wood-burning fireplace, the way we heated our home in the winter. We weren't a family in poverty. To some, we might not have even been considered *poor*. We were undeniably working class. We chopped wood for the fire ourselves, never buying it in those neatly wrapped bundles from the supermarket. That fireplace in the corner of the living room had been how we stayed warm through the winter and it had now become the focal point of what was soon to be Brittany's baby doll crematorium. It was going to serve as the follow through for the threat Dad had just made if Brittany didn't act fast.

Time started moving again.

Brittany, still dodging the inevitable, lingered in the living room, deliberately avoiding the task at hand. Dad finished what he was doing at the kitchen stove and washed his hands at the sink. Without a word, he walked over, picked up the beloved baby doll, looked at Brittany, and said, "I *told you if you didn't pick up your baby doll like your Mom said, I was going to throw it in the fire.*"

Then he opened the wood burning fireplace door, and just like that, in it went.

Brittany screamed. I gasped. Mom kept cleaning like she had seen this coming all along.

Dad? He went back to cooking as if he had just flipped a pancake.

(When you read Lesson 5, "Follow Difficult Conversations with Restorative Ones," you will find out what happened later that day, a classic move from Dad whenever any of *his girls* were upset with him).

There's no doubt Mom had a moment of panic, considering the great lengths she went to in order to get that doll. However, Brittany and I never saw it. It was as if the whole thing had been carefully orchestrated. They operated as one.

As adults, we still hear Mom retell this story, and we now fully understand the epic scolding Dad endured from her later that day. He always half-smiles as she recounts all the details, proud of having supported her, yet at the same time, he shrugs, unable to shake the feeling that still lingers at the thought of one of his girls being upset.

That Christmas morning, there were many lessons we could have taken away, putting your spouse first, supporting yet not overstepping, and following through on your word. The one that rang the loudest and clearest.

*Follow through on your word.*

Following through on what you say is a fundamental principle of integrity, trust, and respect, all qualities our Dad embodied in everything he did. It was how he showed up as a spouse, father, friend, and business partner, as well as to strangers, even when it was not it was always reciprocated.

When words are backed by actions, they carry weight. Dad modeled this for us, proving that staying true to your word matters. Consistently keeping commitments and following through on what you say fosters trust, demonstrating to others that they can depend on you. This is especially crucial in parenting and leadership, where follow-through sets clear expectations and teaches accountability. We knew we could count on Dad to do what he said, even if it led to a smoldering baby doll on Christmas morning.

Whether in small promises or major commitments, following through reinforces character, strengthens relationships, and creates a foundation of trust that lasts far beyond the moment. Follow through on your word and uphold your commitments building a lifetime of trust and confidence in the hearts of those who know you. Of course, if your actions involve tossing a top-tier baby doll into the fire...well, people will remember that too.

# Never Sacrifice Decency for Convenience

*"I said leave."*

One summer afternoon, when I was nine, Mom, Brittany, and I were home when we heard a knock at our front door. This might sound unremarkable but, in our house, the front door was practically ceremonial, reserved for Trick-or-Treaters and the occasional census taker. Everyone who *actually* knew us used the side door under the carport. That was the real entrance. If the glass storm door was unlocked, they would just stroll right in, calling out "Hey y'all anybody home!" as they entered.

When we heard a knock, at the *front* door no less, we knew this was a stranger.

Sure enough, standing on our porch was a man in a button-down shirt and tie, holding a clipboard and wearing the eager expression of someone who had rehearsed his pitch in the mirror that morning. He looked to be in his thirties, and had that vaguely wormy, forgettable look, like a guy you might sit next to on a bus and not even notice until he asked if you wanted to buy a vacuum cleaner.

Which is exactly what he did.

He launched into a breathless spiel about the miracle machine he was selling, something that would "revolutionize the way you clean." (Bold words for a guy who had no idea how seriously Mom took a clean house.)

Mom, ever the Southern hostess even when she didn't want to be, reluctantly let him in, vacuum and all.

What followed was a full-blown performance. He showed her every bell, whistle, and attachment on that dream machine like it was the Swiss Army knife of home sanitation. Then he moved into the dramatic part of the show, dumping mystery debris onto our living room carpet to demonstrate the vacuum's cleaning power.

Another bold move considering that room was more of a museum than a living space. We didn't *use* the formal living room. It was for decoration, and, apparently, now for vacuum demonstrations.

Enter Dad.

The moment he pulled into the driveway he knew something was off. The strange car parked out front could have belonged to anyone but the open front door? That was practically a beacon, like a bat signal, indicating the person inside was not someone we knew.

As Dad stepped in the living room, he took one look at the salesman and the vacuum paraphernalia scattered around then up at Mom to gauge his next move. She gave him *the look*, the one that says, *I'm done here but I'm being polite and he is near the end.* With that Dad promptly turned on his heel in a graceful attempt to escape the sales pitch.

The salesman, ever hopeful, offered a chipper introduction and invited Dad to join the tail end of the presentation.

Dad politely declined in his own subtle way by disappearing into the kitchen and settling into his usual perch: the high-back oak chair at the end of the table, a position from which he could hear everything in the living room without having to engage in any of it.

The salesman launched into the final act of his performance, still unaware that Dad was just a room away, silently listening from his post. Since Mom hadn't already handed over a check for one of his miracle machines, he knew he had to go big or go home and he had no intention of going home empty-handed.

Little did he know, Dad was still very much "in the room," just out of sight and steadily reaching a slow boil after already hearing him ignore Mom's "I am not interested" multiple times.

Determined to make the sale, the salesman ramped up the drama. This time, without visibly tossing anything onto the floor, he made a show of emptying the collection bin to reveal it was pristinely clean. He then vacuumed a fresh section of the already immaculate living room carpet (again, the one we practically were not even supposed to walk on), and with the flair of a magician revealing his final trick, he popped open the bin and showed Mom the debris it had collected.

He delivered this moment like a courtroom revelation: dust, dirt, and drama all in one breathless flourish. "See?" he said, gravely. "This is what your family is living in."

At this point, Mom had already told him, politely but firmly, several times that she wasn't interested. She was reaching the edge of her Southern grace. To a suited up vacuum salesman, she may have still seemed calm. Dad knew the warning signs and it was clear her patience was at a rolling simmer.

The salesman, however, mistook her composure for weakness and leaned in harder. He warned her about the *dangers* of invisible filth, claiming she was putting her family at risk. "Ma'am," he said, "this carpet is practically a petri dish with plush."

What he didn't realize was that his life was about to change.

Dad had been silent long enough. He stood up from his high-back chair and pushed it back with a scrape loud enough to cut through the sales pitch of the vacuum showroom of doom.

"We are not interested. It is time for you to go," he said with the calm intensity of a man who had been raised on respect and had hit his limit.

A normal person would have gathered their belongings and scurried out the door without even winding up the cord of their vacuum. But this guy? He saw one last swirling cyclone of confidence before the motor gave out and he made the critical mistake of saying, "Sir, I just don't think your wife understands how unhealthy this carpet is for your family."

That was it. The last speck of pleasantries got sucked up, what was left of them, anyway.

Dad, short in stature but built like a retired linebacker, stepped forward, grabbed the man by the collar of his button-down shirt and the tie he had so proudly worn to sell salvation in the form of suction and he physically escorted him out the front door. Still speaking calmly but with unmistakable authority, "I said leave," Dad told him. "She said she wasn't interested."

Once they reached the front steps, Dad released him with conviction and tossed the remaining vacuum parts and sales paperwork onto the front lawn like he was scattering grass seed in the fall. Without another word, he closed the door.

Dad didn't hurt the man (though you could tell he had considered it) but his message was as clear as the salesman claimed his HEPA filter would be.

You don't insult his wife to try and make a sale and even deeper than this: you don't elevate yourself by tearing someone else down.

The more Mom rejected his sale the more the salesman tried to shame her. The pitch turned from product to personal, as if humiliation might unlock the checkbook. He was one sentence away from saying he wouldn't let his dog nap on the carpet in our home.

Mom, Brittany, and I have told the story about the day Dad threw the vacuum cleaner salesman out of the house a hundred times over the years but it stuck with me for more than the laugh. It revealed something deeper about Dad. He didn't raise his voice. He didn't curse anyone out or beat them up. He simply stood up and took action making things crystal clear: There's never a good reason to sacrifice decency.

Whether it is the vacuum guy trying to shame his way to a paycheck, a kid on the bus trying to feel big by making someone else feel small, or a coworker climbing the ladder on someone else's shoulders, it's all the same. Dad wouldn't stand for any of it.

He lived with a kind of integrity that didn't seek a spotlight, although we girls couldn't help but shine it on him from time to time. He protected the people he loved, not just from dirt on the carpet but from the kind of ugliness that settles in when people forget their decency.

You don't have to tear others down to build something real, something great.

Kindness and conviction can, and should, exist in the same moment. Bottom line? People matter and Dad never let anyone forget it.

# Show Up How You Want to be Seen

*"I'm not raising girls; I'm raising ladies."*

Our house had more traditional male and female roles but they didn't define us, nor were we defined by them.

I was in sixth grade, eating like a ravenous child, hacking off hunks of food and shoving them in my mouth with complete disregard for how my ogrish eating might affect those around the table. Evidently, Dad had decided I was too old for this. Stopping me mid-bite, he showed me how to cut my food into manageable pieces before saying, *"I'm not raising girls; I'm raising ladies."* Nothing more was said. Dinner continued without issue and those words stayed with me.

*"Your hands are rough. They're not soft like your mom's. Make sure you use that fancy lotion like she does, so they don't end up like mine."* We were sitting in church.  It was

during the Lord's Prayer, we held hands, as we did every Sunday. When it came time to exchange the sign of peace, our family in the front pew would always hug, and Mom and Dad would share a quick kiss, something they did every week. A handshake for those in the pew behind us and a simple smile and a wave for those a little further.

That Sunday was different. When I hugged Dad, he took my hands in his, paused and made that statement to me not as judgment but as a statement of protection. He wanted me to have the choice in how I presented myself and to do this I had to take care of myself and take pride in myself. I could be the hard worker, willing to roll up my sleeves and do anything, just as he had modeled. Or I could be refined, detail-oriented, and intentional, even in something as small as moisturizing my hands. The following Sunday, during the Lord's Prayer I made a point to hold Mom's hand. He was right, hers were the softest hands I had ever felt. They still are.

*"I'm not raising girls; I'm raising ladies."*

That lesson surfaced again when it was time for me to learn to drive. Teaching me was a task Dad took sole responsibility for and his driving school "The Joey Fuqua Driving School" was as unconventional and grueling as you can imagine. It didn't begin behind the wheel of a car. It began with a lawnmower and a three-foot trailer hitched to the back.

If you have ever towed something, you know the shorter the trailer, the harder it is to maneuver. There is little room for correction, every movement must be precise. Dad saw no reason why I should start with a forgiving, full-sized vehicle and trailer when I could learn the *hard* way first. Driving school at every stage elicited an animated and unnecessarily loud coach from Dad. He brought the same passion to his teaching style regardless if we were in a real car on an actual road or crushing dandelions in the back of the acre-and-a-half yard behind our house. Never-the-less, our neighbors always knew when The Joey Fuqua Driving School was in session from the "*Get your head out of your ass!*" and "*Damn It!*" that echoed through our backyard.

Growing up in Tennessee meant we experienced all four seasons and the extreme driving conditions to go along with them. It was a requirement that I learn how to drive in all of them, heavy rain, snow, ice, and high winds. Only when I was confident in all conditions did Dad introduce the next challenge: learning to drive a manual transmission. Here, the lessons started all over again. I earned my driver's license, on a snowy day, no less, but there was one basic lesson I had never been taught and when my husband asked for my hand in marriage, it was as if Dad passed the baton to him.

Dad never officially taught me to pump gas. I had seen him do it. I understood the concept but I had never personally gone through the motions of fueling a vehicle.

The women in our house didn't do it. For years, I thought this was about us, he was "raising ladies" after all, keeping us from getting gas on our hands, sparing us from the weather, or just a way for Dad to cover the expense. As I got older, I realized it was never really about us. It was about him. It was about how he wanted to show up for us, how *he* wanted to be seen. It was a small act of service to his girls, his ladies, and now, it's a legacy that lives on in my husband. We rarely had to tell Dad we needed gas, he just kept our tanks full. If, by chance, we mentioned, he would go before bed to make sure we had a full tank in the morning.

Being a lady, in our house, didn't mean conforming to gender roles, it meant understanding how to show up with intention. Dad knew how to cook, sew, and he did almost all of our ironing. We all worked in the yard, chopped wood, and we weren't afraid to get dirty. He also modeled the importance of showing up when it mattered. Sometimes, that meant dressing for the occasion because of what *we* valued regardless of how others showed up. It meant dropping girls off at the door when it was raining before parking the car. It meant wearing a suit to the funeral, even if others were in jeans.

Dad didn't just raise girls. He didn't just raise ladies. He gave us the tools to be prepared and a gas tank on full to get there. We learned the importance of paying attention to details and to showing up in the world with intention because in the end, how you show up matters. Whether you arrive in heels or work boots with hands that are soft or calloused or whether you're leading the room or supporting from the background, people will remember.

In his way, he taught us that how we show up is how we are perceived, and how we are perceived shapes our impact.

# Follow Difficult Conversations with Restorative Ones.

*"Don't make me put a foot up your ass."*

As a parent, setting boundaries and dishing out consequences when your kids decide to test the limits are all just part of the job description. It's the stuff that gives you a fighting chance at raising productive citizens who, hopefully, don't turn into serial offenders of the "ungrateful teen" handbook.

Dad wasn't the loudest disciplinarian in our house but we never questioned his expectations. He was not the kind of parent you were scared of and he didn't come storming into the room with steam coming out of his ears (*usually*). When we crossed the line, we knew it, he made sure of it.

Being sassy was practically a sport for my sister and me in our early teenage years. Honestly, we weren't any mouthier than your average teen but with Dad there was no such thing as just letting that one slide. If we backtalked Mom or got "a little too big for our britches," Dad called us on it. Every. Single. Time. Not in a casual, "Hey, don't say that again" kind of way but in a very direct, "Mouth off like that again and you're gonna get a foot up your ass" kind of way.

No, he never actually did it. *"Don't make me put a foot up your ass."* was as common a phrase used in our house during those years as "Wash your hands" might have been in someone else's home.   Looking back, I'm pretty sure both he and Mom counted our steadily declining sass levels as a major parenting victory.

Dad couldn't just leave his discipline tactics to sit with us though. At some point later in the same day, he'd snuggle up to us sheepishly let us know he "wasn't trying to be mean" and he'd make sure we weren't still mad at him. Peace and harmony in the house was paramount to him and the mere *thought* that someone was upset sent him into a stuttering parenting mess... even if he was 100% in the right. He could've been the star of his own soap opera titled "Dad's Guilt Trip."

Being sassy may have been the leading cause of correction in our house but sometimes outright defiance took center stage and those moments earned a bit more attention from our parents.

Brittany had always been the edgier one, the one who liked to test the boundaries, even if it resulted in charred baby dolls. While our Dad wasn't big on superstitions, there were a few non-negotiable rules he followed for example the person who opened a pocket knife *had* to close it and you never gave someone a wallet without money in it. The most important to him was that you *always* ate black-eyed peas and hog jowl on New Year's Day for good luck and prosperity. These weren't just suggestions; they were essentially commandments in our house.

We all knew the rules. We grew up with them. Until one fateful New Year's Day Brittany decided she was *not* eating black-eyed peas. Not one bite. Not even a lonely pea for show. She wasn't even going to play the game and pretend.

There we were, gathered around our square maple kitchen table, practically willing Brittany to *just eat one bite*. She wasn't having it. No amount of peer pressure, pleading, or logic was going to change her mind. It was like we were trying to convince a brick wall to join us for a family vacation.

This, of course, did *not* go over well with Dad. He insisted, *one bite*. After a lengthy back-and-forth that felt more like a hostage negotiation than a family dinner, Dad drew his infamous line in the sand:

"If you don't eat a bite of those peas now, you'll sit here until you do."

Sure enough, the bowl sat on the table as a silent reminder of the epic black-eyed pea standoff. Hours later, Brittany still hadn't budged, now asleep at the kitchen table, likely dreaming of a world where black eyed peas were banned from family dinners. Dad couldn't just leave things hanging. He woke her, softened his tone and let her know he loved her. He explained, yet again, why the one bite mattered. After all, *this is just what you do on New Year's*

*Day.* It was about more than black eyed peas, you were tempting fate, gambling with destiny, courting disaster.

In the end, Brittany caved. She took her obligatory bite, peace was restored, and Dad sealed the deal with an ice cream cone. When things got heated, Dad paired his restorative conversations with peace offerings: ice cream, candy, flowers, whatever fit the moment. It wasn't about the treat itself; it was his way of saying, "Hey, *that got a little intense but we're good now.*" It was emotional first aid with a scoop of vanilla on top.

They say some of the fondest memories are made around the dinner table. I'm not sure *fond* is the word I would use for that New Year's memory but it was definitely one we'll never forget.

Dad's follow-up chats might have seemed like creampuff moments, a sign of weakness even, but as we got older, we realized it was quite the opposite. It takes real strength to circle back after a tough conversation and restore the relationship, even when it is to a four-year-old for throwing her doll in the fire on Christmas morning or the preteen who refused her peas for prosperity. It takes more courage to lean in after a difficult conversation than to simply stand your ground and leave the tension hanging in the air like a forgotten holiday decoration.

Dad's disciplinary diplomacy taught us setting boundaries is important and following those boundaries with love and authentic restoration, was what truly leaves a mark. He showed us that it is okay to have difficult conversations, necessary in fact, but it is equally important to follow them up with restorative ones. You don't have to be right to make things right and sometimes, a well-timed ice cream cone is exactly what it takes to turn a tough moment into a treasured memory.

# Be Confident

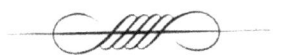

*"You don't have to like it; you just have to do it."*

We were always comfortable with who we were and where we came from. A generous helping of humility with a side of quiet confidence was how our family operated. No matter how sure of yourself you are, life has a way of shaking that confidence. Sometimes it's shallow moments like a wardrobe malfunction or tripping in public; other times, it's deeper wounds like rejection or facing the unknown. Regardless of the source, those moments can leave you feeling as unsteady as a toddler on roller skates.

Our family wasn't exempt from confidence-shaking experiences. As kids of two working parents, my sister and I rode the bus home from school once we were old enough to stay home alone. As both a bus rider and now a school principal, school buses were and still are the wild west of the transportation world. My late middle school experience was a prime example of that. Every afternoon, a girl a couple of years older than me would shout derogatory names from the back of the bus as I walked down the aisle to get off at my stop. I had no idea what those words meant; I didn't even know half of them were actual insults but I knew one thing for sure: they weren't good. Her taunts were so effective that they caused me to sink into my seat and ultimately beg my parents to let me go back to aftercare just to avoid the daily humiliation.

Once they learned the real reason I wanted off the bus, they were beyond irritated and determined to provide a space for the situation to be rectified. We lived in a small town, so their actions led to one of the more awkward Saturdays I had encountered. There was a knock on our door and there stood the bus bully herself, at *my house*, ready to apologize. Was it uncomfortable? Absolutely. Did it challenge my confidence? You bet it did. Instead of retreating into my shell, I leaned into that awkwardness and allowed the moment to unfold.

She apologized, while standing in the doorway of my Little Mermaid themed bedroom as "Under the Sea" played on my boombox. I could see her Mom waiting with crossed arms in the front room of our house as she chatted with mine. This gave me every indication the apology would likely not carry much further than the moment we were in making my next bus ride even more difficult. I couldn't have been more wrong. That day was the last time she ever spoke of the terrible things she would say to me.

My bus rides became much more pleasant. It was more than just confronting the discomfort, it was the result of something we had been taught: when life shakes you up, the best way to steady yourself is to lean in and find your footing, even if it feels like you're stumbling through the process.

Dad was our shirtless, cutoff-overalls-wearing role model for this confidence. No one "leaned in" quite like he did, especially from the perch of his trusty riding lawnmower. His mower was more than just a grass cutting machine, it was a mobile command center. It doubled as a lawn tractor to haul water to the garden, firewood to the house, grass clippings to the burn pile, and vegetables back from the garden (you see where his priorities were). It even doubled as Dad's personal transportation to visit our neighbors, Mr. Raymond and Mrs. Ann, where they would sit in the garage, look out into the back yard, enjoy a beer or two, and swap garden treasures after supper each evening. It was an essential part of our summertime routine, right up there with family dinners and making sure Dad's lawnmower hadn't backfired into the neighbor's doghouse.

*Mr. Raymond sitting in his garage looking over at our yard.*

*Mr. Raymond and Dad*

Because we were a "make the dollar stretch" kind of family, Dad's Green John Deere was a Frankenstein of lawn mowers. It had character, lots of character. Duct tape held together cracks from past collisions with trees, a strategic move to reduce the amount of weed-eating required later. The epoxy patchwork left the mower looking like a patchy quilt of mismatched green hues, as if it had been assembled during a particularly wild art class. The real showstopper was the sound, the bang that followed every time Dad turned the mower off. The backfire was so loud, it could've been mistaken for a shotgun blast and it never failed to startle anyone within a mile radius. Instead of being embarrassed, Dad embraced it. The backfire would happen about eight seconds after he turned the mower off, giving him ample time to step off, striking a dramatic pose (like a wizard casting a spell). He would hold one arm outstretched while bending one over his head, waiting for the inevitable BOOM. Then, without missing a beat, he'd go right back to whatever he was doing, as though nothing had happened. It was his way of controlling the uncontrollable, of grounding himself in confidence instead of succumbing to the embarrassment of his own lawnmower's midlife crisis.

Dad knew life would throw us more than just loud lawnmowers and school bus bullies. Perhaps he understood that our upbringing, full of hard work, field parties, and less-than-perfect grammar, might one day, potentially, leave us feeling out of place walking into ritzy country clubs, attending elegant dinner parties, and sitting in professional spaces surrounded by people who could pronounce all their words correctly with impeccable grammar. His playful resilience demonstrated how to lean in, steady yourself, and find your confidence in the chaos when you're knocked off balance.

True confidence is about facing discomfort and uncertainty head-on. It's about acknowledging the shaky moments and trusting yourself to stand firm anyway. Whether it's an awkward apology, an intimidating new opportunity, or a lawnmower that sounds like it's launching a small military coup, the key is to lean in, embrace the unknown, and let those moments build a deeper, stronger confidence within you.

# Find Peace in Nature

*"I'm going to die eating good food."*

Fish, frogs, deer, and duck, they were so much more than the animals Dad hunted. His appreciation for nature and the gifts it provided was seen in the way he navigated hunting. He had a rule: you only killed what you would eat. For Dad, this wasn't just a practical guideline, it was a demonstration of reverence. He believed taking from nature meant taking responsibility and he lived by that principle. His hunting approach ultimately became a lesson in respect and understanding that nature's gifts were to be appreciated, not taken for granted.

Of all the things he caught and hunted, fish were hands down his favorite to eat. Naturally, when we were younger and funds were tighter, fishing was far less of a sport and much more of a job. We would all load up in his pickup truck and head to his favorite fishing spots. Brittany and I would "fish" with Mom while Dad always managed to find a spot with plenty of distance between us. He had standards, of course. He preferred Bluegill, Bass, and Stripe, so if we caught something else, we had to be very careful removing the hook so we could throw it back without harming it.

Later, when finances were much more stable and fruitful, Dad's survival instinct when it came to fishing did not change. He now has a couple different fishing boats to choose from and a place on the Kentucky Lake section of the Tennessee River, revered for excellent Bass fishing, his favorite, but when you fish with Dad it is still a serious operation. His side of the boat is the side that matters, the only end he is concerned about. It does not matter if your side of the boat has no trees in sight and a perfect little spot just waiting for a cast.  If Dad's side had one stubborn fish that hasn't moved in 20 minutes, that's where he is staying and, well you are on your own.

You may end up tangled in tree limbs, have to reel up your line multiple times to stay off the rocks, or just sit tight until you can cast because Dad will always have his eye on the prize, catching fish to fill the freezer. In Dad's mind, every trip was a strategic mission and if that meant the rest of us spent half the afternoon doing more line management than actual fishing it was a sacrifice worth making.  After all, the freezer space didn't fill itself.

Fishing with Dad also meant accepting that his way was the *right way*. One of the many reasons why we decided his grandparent name would be, "Boss."  If you cast it in the wrong spot, he'd give you the look, the one that silently asked, "What exactly are you trying to accomplish here?" If you snagged your line, you would hear him muttering under his breath like a man whose patience had been worn thin by both bad fishing and a subpar fishing companion. Heaven help you if you didn't get the net quick enough when he was reeling in a big one, Dad acted like the family might go hungry because of you. Despite all of this, he never had a shortage of fishing buddies, they all shared similar stories. God bless my mom for trying to warn them. She still remains Dad's number-one fishing partner, tackle box in hand enduring every shenanigan with the grace of a seasoned pro.

From the shore or a boat, fishing would take up the majority of our day growing up and when we returned home, Dad would "clean" the fish. Carefully removing the skin, head, tails, and filleting off the meat from each side, he would toss the fillets in a bowl of ice. Mom would then package it all up in serving-size portions filled with ice-cold water to be frozen and enjoyed later. Dad never cleaned fish and ate them on the same day, his appetite for fish was dramatically diminished after spending hours preparing them. Any day after, though, he was ready to enjoy them, always fried, never grilled or baked. Mom certainly makes the best fried fish, he would say, and he'd promptly acknowledge that it wasn't the healthiest way to eat them by adding, "If I'm going to die, I'm going to die eating good food."

Dad always loved good food and he had no shame in eating it exactly the way he wanted.

Frog gigging was a sport he did not engage in regularly or much past our elementary school years but when he did, he was sure to make sure we knew what a delicacy we had in frog legs. Cleaning them was a "princess moment" for me, a title I wore proudly. I was Dad's helper in all things and that included being his self-appointed assistant when it was time to prepare the frog legs he had caught. My job? I had to reach down in the bucket and grab the chosen frog for Dad to prepare. Before handing it over, I'd give it a quick smooch, just to make sure it wasn't the next Prince Charming.

Of course, the frogs didn't seem quite as amused by this process. On occasion, one would have enough life left in it to give a powerful kick that would send me shrieking and tossing it back in the bucket like I was playing a high-stakes game of hot potato. Dad would laugh, shaking his head, grinning like he knew it was all part of the show.

As he skinned and prepared the legs to be fried up for that night's meal, we'd talk about the beautiful colors that could be seen in their skin, an appreciation for the beauty in them, even though they would later be dinner. In those moments, watching the shimmer of greens and browns on a frog's skin I was learning, without even realizing it, how to respect the wild and find beauty in its complexity.

Deer hunting was a conflicting sport for Dad, and I picked up on that early due to his deep love and appreciation for nature. He didn't like deer meat, at all. In fact, he would wrinkle his nose at the thought of it like he had just smelled sour milk but he believed in only killing what you planned to eat, so he was determined to figure out a way to make it palatable. After all, "he was going to die eating good food," and deer meat didn't exactly fit the bill. "Too gamey and too lean, no fat!" he would say. He eventually mastered the art of making some of the best Deer jerky on this side of the Mississippi. It was a tedious and time-consuming process that involved slicing, soaking for hours-days, seasoning, and dehydrating. His homemade jerky became a prized snack and a welcome change from our usual pickles and salsa made fresh from the garden. In our house, jerky was currency. Need a favor? Offer some jerky. Want to borrow something from a friend or neighbor? Better bring jerky. The stuff had power.

Despite his jerky success, Dad's admiration for nature and the beauty of deer ultimately outweighed his desire to keep up his side hustle as the leading jerky chef in town. Once he discovered photography, his rifle was replaced with a Canon camera and several rolls of film. He still went on deer hunting trips with his buddies but now he shot with a lens instead of a bullet. I imagine his hunting friends had a good laugh watching him crouched behind a tree with his camera like some sort of National Geographic intern whispering excitedly about the perfect shot.

*Dad and me on the tailgate with a prized buck.*

Those moments became less about filling the freezer and more about filling his heart with gratitude for the beauty of the natural world. He found that just as satisfying as a perfect batch of jerky.

Duck hunting was different altogether. While many duck hunters, like Dad, are blue-collar workers, it was considered more of a rich man's sport. The expense of waders, decoys, duck blinds, and boats had kept Dad from the hobby until later in life. On a guided fishing trip, Dad met two brothers, James and Brad, who were avid duck hunters. From there he paid to go on a couple of guided duck-hunting trips and just like that, the "Duck Boys" became a trio with Dad.

Every weekend during duck season, Dad and the Duck Boys hunted together. If they had a large group going for a guided trip, Dad would go as the "duck blind cook." I think he came to love this role more than the actual hunt itself. He got to enjoy all the beauty of nature and his love for cooking wrapped into one. The only problem: as his family, we were subjected to countless inventive culinary concoctions. With limited cooking surfaces in the duck blind and his desire to "eat good food," Dad had to get creative.

We endured questionable recipes, particularly when it came to desserts, not his forte in a normal kitchen let alone a duck blind. His creativity reached its peak with what he proudly dubbed "Duck Blind Delight," a dessert that, after four attempts, made us unanimously refuse to serve as the duck blind taste testers for any more of his culinary experiments. We still aren't sure what was in the gelatinous fourth version but I'm confident THAT constancy was not the desired outcome.

He didn't like to eat duck one bit but the Duck Boys loved it. It was a five-star partnership.

Duck hunting became Dad's newest nature obsession. The number of books about migratory birds and Tennessee

River waterfowl in his tiny half bath (barely big enough to turn around in and certainly not large enough to bend over in) quickly outnumbered the ones identifying fish in the Tennessee River, his favorite place to both duck hunt and fish. He would light up telling us about the different color variations on the ducks and how they looked different when flying versus when they landed on the water.

At this stage in his life, he and Mom owned a house on Kentucky Lake, making it very convenient for him to duck hunt every weekend during the season. When not hunting, they spent the rest of the year Bass fishing together. Much to Dad's delight, the property that ran adjacent to theirs was a state-owned wildlife refuge. He loved this place and would ride us around pointing out the various ducks. Brittany and I had children of our own by this point and when they were very little, they were enthusiastic about spotting his ducks and using the duck calls. As they grew older, their enthusiasm waned but Dad's never did. His love and appreciation for nature never faded. I suspect he still took just as much joy in pointing out the ducks as he did when he first started, even if his audience was not quite as captivated as they once were.

He and Mom taught us to appreciate the gifts of the earth, and Dad fostered a sense of wonder and respect for nature that helped us slow down and treasure the present moment. Finding peace in nature isn't just about admiring the beauty of a sunset or the changing leaves, it's about finding peace and gratitude in the world around you. Nature has a way reminding us that life moves forward and beauty can be found even in life's simplest moments. On hard days or when I'm sad or upset, I find myself yearning to be outside, to be grounded in the gifts nature provides. Somehow, that seems to steady me more than anything else. Am I a hunter? Nope. Do I bait a hook or take a fish off the line like Mom? Absolutely not. I can, however, find complete and total solace sitting on the back porch, digging in the dirt, picking flowers, or even pulling a few weeds and I find no better sound to wake up to than birds chirping in the morning. Perhaps that is because our simple, wise Dad knew all along that developing an appreciation for nature was more than a pastime, it was a way to find peace when life gets rocky. He saw the beauty in each fish, frog leg, deer, and duck. He showed us how to enjoy nature and gave us a lifelong refuge in it.

# Friendships Can Start Anywhere

Before Dad opened his own shop in the small town where we lived, he worked in a subsection of Nashville, Tennessee, until I was in late middle school. He had worked at this same transmission shop in Nashville since he was in high school. He seemingly knew everyone in the entire subsection of Nashville where the shop was located.

When I say Dad never met a stranger, I mean it in the most literal sense. To this day, people have to find creative and polite ways to escape conversations with him. Variations of *"Well, it was great seeing you but I really have to go..."* have been uttered so often they might as well be printed on a farewell plaque in his honor.

One particular summer day, when Brittany and I were in elementary school we found ourselves stationed in the transmission shop's tiny office. We set up with sticker books, arts and crafts, and a snack stash that could rival a doomsday prepper's pantry. From our perch by the window, we had prime viewing of the busy Nashville street outside, watching the steady flow of passersby and the occasional confused pedestrian who wandered in needing directions.

The office had its usual scent, a fine bouquet of transmission fluid with a hint of cigar smoke, courtesy of Bobby, the shop owner. Bobby operated the front desk with a cigar perpetually dangling from his mouth as he juggled phone calls on a landline with a coiled cord so long it could've doubled as a jump rope. The mechanics popped in periodically, usually to ask us deeply philosophical questions like how many boyfriends we had, which was both hilarious and wildly inaccurate given that our only true loves at the time were Lisa Frank sticker books and watching Alf on Monday Nights.

Shortly after lunch, a big city bus pulled up out front and off stepped a man unlike anyone we had ever seen in our small town. He was tall and thin, with jet-black hair streaked with silver and skin as deep and rich as the night sky. When he smiled, his teeth glowed so bright and flawless they could have starred in their own toothpaste commercial. He greeted Brittany and me warmly before making a beeline for the restroom, the very same one we had already visited about *a hundred times* already that day.

See, the shop had a water dispenser with those tiny cone-shaped paper cups. To us they were the most exciting thing since Saturday morning cartoons. We were fascinated. Dad told us we *couldn't waste them*, so instead of getting a new cup each time, we would carefully reuse our little paper chalices, taking turns refilling them inevitably needing the bathroom at an unprecedented rate.

Dad came into the office while the mysterious city bus man was still in the restroom. Brittany and I sat there, still processing the disruption of our sacred water-drinking routine, when the man finally emerged. Dad greeted him with his usual enthusiasm.

"*How's it going, Jimmy?!*" he bellowed, clapping the man on the back before pulling him into one of those classic Dad-style half-hugs.

Just like that, the mystery was solved. *Of course*, this man was Dad's friend. *Everyone* was Dad's friend. Strangers? Never heard of them. He could meet someone for the first time and still act like they had been swapping Christmas cards for years.

Dad turned to us with a grin. "*Girls, this is my friend Jimmy.*"

We nodded knowingly. If a person had ever stood within a five-foot radius of our father, they were by default his lifelong companion.

Dad launched into a full explanation of why we were hanging out at the transmission shop that day as if Jimmy had been dying to know the intricate details of our summer childcare arrangements. Instead of politely nodding and moving on, Jimmy did something unexpected. Without hesitation, he turned to Dad and said, *"You think they'd like to go for a ride on the bus?"*

Wait. Hold on. Did he just say *ride on the bus*?

Jimmy explained that his loop around the city would take about an hour and before Brittany and I could even process the excitement, Dad turned to us.

*"Girls, you wanna go ride Mr. Jimmy's big bus around the city?"*

Did we *want* to?! Was that even a real question? We nodded so fast we nearly gave ourselves whiplash.

With snacks in hand, we followed Mr. Jimmy outside and climbed aboard the biggest coolest vehicle we had ever been allowed to ride and without an adult hovering over us for the first time in our young lives.

Mr. Jimmy showed us where to sit, right up front on the first seat, the VIP section of public transit, if you will. Then, just like that, we were off, rolling through the city with a front-row view of the action, watching passengers come and go as Jimmy greeted each one like an old friend.

For an hour, we weren't just two kids stuck at a transmission shop on a summer day, we were adventurers on a grand urban expedition. We saw places we had never noticed before and waved at strangers like we were on a parade float. Soaking in the simple magic of something as ordinary, yet extraordinary, as a city bus ride felt like a new chapter in a story we didn't know we were part of as passengers shuffled on and off at each stop.

After a full loop around the city, Mr. Jimmy pulled back up to the shop on Hillsboro Circle and delivered us safely back, like a chauffeur dropping off his tiny VIP passengers.

That day, we learned an important lesson: the best adventures come from the most unexpected invitations and sometimes, your Dad's *never-met-a-stranger* personality brings the most incredible people into your life, like a kind city bus driver who turned a regular summer day into a memory we would never forget. Although it may have been one our Mom had a thing or two to say about that evening. "You let them do WHAT!"

Friendships don't have to fit the mold we're accustomed to. They don't have to come from our usual circles. That summer day at the transmission shop, Dad taught us that firsthand, by simply *being himself* he demonstrated how friendships can start anywhere. It was a Mr. Rogers moment in his own way.

Mr. Jimmy, a city bus driver, didn't fit the typical mold of friendship for our small-town world. He was from far outside the little town where we lived and he crossed an invisible racial barrier we didn't even know existed. Mr. Jimmy was a Black man and we were two young White girls from a small town that was 99.9% White. We had little experience with people who didn't look like us and many people in our community at the time might not have looked very kindly toward our Dad for putting us on a city bus with a Black man. That didn't matter to him. He saw Mr. Jimmy as a friend first. Yes, a Black man and a city bus driver but above all he was a friend and that was the title that meant the most.

Many lessons could be derived from that day. Don't judge someone by their appearance or by what they can offer or it is important to be open to friendships wherever life takes you. While those are true, the most powerful one I took away was even simpler: *Friends can be found anywhere.*

They don't have to look like us, act like us, or share the same background, religion, nationality, political beliefs, or traditions. Friendship isn't about checking off a list of similarities. It's about finding those moments of connection, those shared laughs, those unspoken understandings that bridge any perceived differences. Whether it's over a common interest, a shared experience, or just a mutual appreciation for a good conversation, friendship has a way of weaving itself into our lives when we least expect it.

The best friendships? The ones that don't fit neatly into any category, the ones that span different circles, cross invisible boundaries, and exist in places you never thought to look, those are the friendships that don't just bless you. They *change* you by opening your world and broadening your perspective.

That day, we thought we were just two kids riding a city bus for fun. Looking back, we were learning something far more valuable: If you keep your heart open, if you let curiosity and kindness guide you, you will find friends in the most unexpected places. When you do, your world will never be small again. Go look for friends and don't ever be closed off to the possibility of meeting a new one.

# Say Sorry Without Hesitation

*"Some of the biggest business deals are made on a golf course."*

Our mom worked in Nashville, which was about a 45-minute commute to and from work for her each day. Dad had built a thriving transmission business in our small town, affording him the opportunity to work five minutes from our home by the time Brittany was in middle school and I was in high school. This proximity between work and home also gave him the flexibility to serve as our chauffeur from after-school events before we could drive ourselves.

With me, this was not much of an imposition and did not require too many invites to his calendar or colorful schedule boards to keep track of everything. I wasn't involved in a lot of extracurricular activities. One year I tried cross country for the sole purpose of being with my middle school bestie, whose mom took us home after practice. I played golf in high school because Dad said it was important for me to learn "some of the biggest business deals are made on a golf course," and honestly, I thought the outfits were cute. We carpooled to the golf course and one of my teammates passed right by our house, so she dropped me off on her way home until I was able to drive.

Brittany, on the other hand, was involved in EVERYTHING, beginning in early middle school and continuing through her senior year of high school. She did cheerleading, took tumbling lessons, played tennis, and of course, played golf "because everyone needed to learn how to swing a golf club." There was rarely a day that she didn't have somewhere to be after school. As a business owner, this meant sometimes Dad would get stuck with a customer and one of his employees, who he always treated like family, would run to pick up Brittany from whatever practice she was at that afternoon.

Between this and the fact that Dad would often pick her up as he was test-driving a car, Brittany had to be on her toes. There was zero predictability in the vehicle she was going to be picked up in from day to day. Dad fixed the transmission in virtually every vehicle you could imagine and we were subjected to being picked up in them or having them sit in our driveway overnight if the parking lot of his shop was too full. You name it, police cars, hearses, El Caminos, dump trucks, run-of-the-mill cars and trucks, fancy convertibles, limos, nothing was off limits. If it had four wheels and needed transmission work, it seemed destined to make an appearance in our driveway at some point. It was like living at a used car dealership, except none of the cars were for sale and all of them were in questionable mechanical condition, until he was finished with them.

If there was one constant in Brittany's unpredictable chauffeur service, it was that Dad never picked her up quietly. Whether he was idling in a tow truck or rolling up in a Mustang with the top down that sounded like it belonged in a NASCAR pit stop, his arrival was rarely subtle. This particular week, during Brittany's freshman year of high school, there were no outrageous vehicles to pick her up from cheer practice but Dad did forget her one day. He got caught up on a project at work and lost track of time. This meant neither he nor one of the guys from the shop showed up at the designated time practice was over that day. Brittany waited until she had to call and remind him to come get her.

Later that same week, when it came time for another cheer practice day, Brittany was taking no chances. She launched into her morning reminder to Dad, regaling him with all the details: time, place, exact pickup location, just shy of drawing him a map and setting an alarm on his phone. Dad, who was elbow-deep in ground beef preparing burgers for dinner, finally cut her off the second time she started down her detailed timeline. "I GOT IT! I know what time to be there!" Dad barked with a wave of his hamburger-stained hand.

Brittany rolled her eyes at him, a bold move in our household. Big mistake. That sent him into orbit and without missing a beat, Dad grabbed a fistful of raw hamburger meat and hurled it across the kitchen in her direction. Luckily, his aim wasn't great and the hunk of meat smacked the living room wall with a thud so loud it echoed through the house. Brittany, never one to let a good zinger go to waste, turned and deadpanned, "If that had hit me, it could have killed me." With that, she grabbed her bag and walked out the door to catch her ride to school.

Knowing Dad and how sensitive he was to us being upset with him, I can only imagine what the rest of his morning looked like: fuming at Brittany's audacious eye roll and stewing in regret for losing his cool, the meat cleanup must have added further insult to injury. For Dad, this was one of those moments that required a follow-up conversation and it needed to start with an "I'm sorry." Dad knew he didn't have to be the first one in the wrong to make the first right move.

That day, Brittany received a dozen red roses and a bouquet of balloons at her high school with a note reading, "I'm Sorry, Love You, Dad." As you can imagine, everyone from the office staff to janitors and every student from the freshman to the senior class wanted to know who sent Brittany such an extravagant gift to school. It seemed like a declaration of undying love.

When Brittany revealed the truth, that the roses and balloons were from her Dad, the curiosity only deepened. "What did you *do*?" people asked, like she was some kind of criminal mastermind. It wasn't even close to her birthday. Brittany retold the story of their morning spat, complete with dramatic flair and hand gestures, and how a wad of raw hamburger meat had sailed through the air in her direction.

It didn't take long for the whole ordeal to be dubbed "The Meatball Incident," a title that spread through the halls like an expertly played game of teenage telephone. The name "Meatball" clung to Brittany for weeks. Her friends would greet her in the cafeteria with exaggerated Italian accents, shouting "Hey, Meat-a-ball!" in their best Mario and Luigi impressions. The nickname stuck for quite a while, much to Dad's chagrin. He took it in stride though, as did Brittany.  I am sure deep down it was mortifying for him. He had spent years building a reputation as the laid-back, everyone's-favorite Dad, the one who always volunteered for school events and grilled burgers for fundraisers.  He had a magic way of keeping a crowd of rowdy teenagers in line with just a smile and befriending us all through his antics. He was now "The Meatball Guy." Honestly, people laughed it off because this moment was so wildly out of character for him.  It just took him a little more time to be able to laugh with them.

That afternoon, Dad wasn't late to pick Brittany up from cheer practice. I imagine he was early, even in his own vehicle, just to be safe. Brittany emerged from practice carrying her roses and balloons, her public apology for the morning's "meatball mayhem." The scene had a real "final scene of a sitcom" vibe, order was restored, harmony was back in place, Dad was at peace, Brittany was smiling again, and most importantly, she wasn't mad at him.

When Mom returned home from work that evening, there was a nice bouquet of red roses on the table that weren't for her and a dinner time story that would have been even better told over spaghetti and meatballs instead of hamburgers. Dad was always so good at saying sorry and it didn't matter who was around to hear it. He regularly modeled the art of apologizing. He didn't hesitate to say sorry because he knew it made two people instantly feel better: the one apologizing and the one on the receiving end. He never waited for the other person to say sorry first, even if they were the one who started it, or if their mistake was bigger. Relationships mattered more than keeping score. His final lesson in apologizing? They don't always have to be private. Sure, for deeply personal matters, a private apology may be more appropriate. Sometimes, a public apology can do more, it shows ownership of the mistake and validates those affected because mistakes happen, even if they involve airborne hamburger meat.

# Jealousy has No Place in Relationships

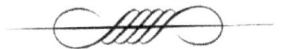

*"Can you call your momma?"*

Saturday mornings in our house were sacred. The moment we woke up, Brittany and I would head straight for Mom's bed, not to snuggle under the covers but to perch cross-legged atop them and launch into the latest chatter. A ritual as predictable as the sunrise. There were always crumbs in the bed, the occasional spilled OJ, and holiday sales ads strewn across the comforter but none of it ever mattered.

If we had a sleepover, our friends simply assimilated into the tradition like it was a requirement of friendship. If you were in our house on a Saturday morning, you were part of the bed-bound board meeting.

Ever the accommodating host, Mom would push herself up against the headboard wiping sleep from her eyes while giving a slow, drawn-out "morning" to her new roommates before executing her weekly command: "Joey, coffee!"

Programmed by years of practice, Dad would sit at the kitchen table in one of the tall ladder-back chairs, newspaper open, shirt notably absent, clad only in his usual morning navy shorts. He never rushed breakfast. If you were starving when he started, you'd be a full-blown philosopher contemplating the meaning of life by the time he finished. One to two hours is not unheard of for a simple breakfast of sausage or bacon and eggs with toast. The smell of bacon or sausage would already be working its way through our three-bedroom ranch-style home, teasing our empty stomachs with promises of an eventual breakfast.

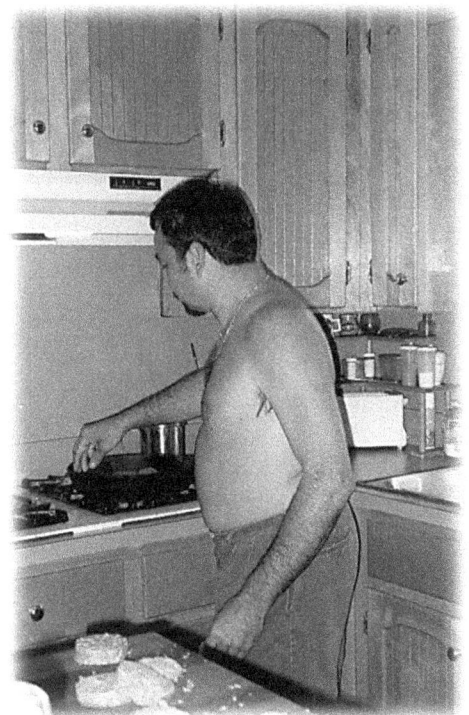

*Dad making breakfast in his classic blue morning shorts—shirtless and taking his time.*

Mom's command for coffee was less of a request and more of a royal decree. To Dad, it always seemed to register as an invitation rather than an order. He would arrive in the bedroom, coffee in hand, with a self-satisfied look, as if he had personally roasted and brewed the beans himself.

After delivering the coffee, he would inevitably have something to share from the newspaper, usually a comic strip or some bizarre headline that he found hilarious. Without fail, he would ask if any of "his other girls" wanted anything. This was an offering for all the girls who were currently making "his GIRL", our mom, so happy in this moment. It was not a limited offer for just Brittany and me, this was an all-inclusive, VIP service for every girl currently propping up pillows alongside Mom. It never had to be explained. If you were there, you were included.

Our drink orders would come rapid-fire, juice, chocolate milk, hot cocoa, tea, you name it. If we spoke too quickly, he would feign confusion, cocking his head and making us repeat ourselves slower, like he was processing complex mathematical equations. Everything was a game with him.

When he returned, drinks in hand, he never simply handed them over. He had to make an entrance lingering just long enough to lean over the bed and deliver a well-placed toe pull or a quick swipe down the bottom of someone's foot, causing an eruption of squeals and protests. It was his way of inserting himself into our morning without hijacking it. Mom had her girls. Dad was just the playful interloper, the mischievous coffee delivery man whose presence was always felt but never dared to overshadow the queen of the bed.

Each Saturday morning unfolded like the one before it: full of laughter, lazy conversation, caffeine, and crumbs. It was tradition and it was ours.

Dad understood something important and we had a front row seat to a valuable life lesson, strong relationships don't have room for jealousy. He reinforced what Mom had with us, nurtured it even in his own playful way. He understood the foundation of a loving family wasn't about competing for attention but about ensuring that each bond was cherished and strengthened. His role on those Saturday mornings was to be the steady presence that made the ritual even more special. In doing so, he didn't just support our connection with Mom, it deepened our connection with him, as well.

Never one to upset his girls (if he could avoid it) Dad had a knack for using the mother-daughter bond he had so openly fostered to his advantage in two key ways. I first recognized the strategy of this approach when I was a teenager. I had a long-term boyfriend and one evening he was allowed to stay past the time my parents went to bed. We cozied up on the sofa to watch a movie, completely unaware that Dad would soon be making an unexpected appearance.

At some point, he shuffled into the living room after getting a glass of water. Dad saw us laying on the sofa all cozied up, paused, asked what we were watching and then *nothing*. Not a word, not a look of disapproval, just a simple nod before heading back to bed. Seemed like he was fine with it, right?

Wrong.

The next day, it was Mom who delivered the message. "You don't need to be laying on the sofa with boys. It is the same reason they aren't allowed in your bedroom." She followed up with, "If you do that again, you will send your Dad stuttering into next year." We often teased that Dad would stutter when he was upset about something. In reality, it wasn't a stutter.  It was more of an internal buffering process, a desperate attempt to phrase things in a way that got his point across without anyone being mad at him and Mom seemed to always be the translator of his good intentions.

Instead of awkwardly confronting the situation himself and perhaps stuttering through it he funneled his feelings through Mom.  He trusted her words would carry the weight of his concern without the burden of his anxiety. He wasn't avoiding conflict; he was navigating it with the precision of a man who understood that the strongest relationships are built on respect and understanding not on dominance and demands.

The second time I saw Dad leverage the relationship we had with Mom, I was a mother to a teenager myself. Dad desperately wanted mom to attend an event with him. He had been trying for weeks to convince her it was a great idea but no matter how he pitched it, she shot it down. She wasn't listening. She wasn't budging. So, he called me.

"Alisha, I need your help with mom. You could tell her to paint the house neon green and she would think it was a good idea." He went on, "If anyone can convince her, it's you, and I just really need her to do this. Can you see if you can get her on board? If you sell it as a good idea, she will think it's a good one too."

Of course, I called Mom. After a casual chat, I brought up the infamous event Dad so desperately was trying to get Mom to attend with him. She rattled off her reasons for standing firm, laying out her rock-solid case. I listened, threw in a few "I wonder" questions, and planted a few strategic seeds along the way. By the end of the conversation, she had a new idea, a brilliant one, in fact. She was going to go along with Dad's plan, go to the event, and better yet, she had her own helpful agenda in doing so.

"Great idea, Mom!" I said, trying not to laugh.

Dad knew exactly what he was doing. He understood that real love doesn't breed jealousy, it nurtures connection. He never resented the fact that we called Mom every day and him once a week, at best. He wasn't annoyed that Mom seemed to trust the advice of her children over her husband's infinite wisdom. He didn't get insecure about the relationships she had with others, whether it was us girls, her friends, or even her so-called "work husband." He leaned into it. He saw the strength in the relationships she built and embraced them because they weren't just good for her, they were good for him, too.

They provided love, comfort, friendship, help, and security for them both, whatever the situation called for there seemed to be someone they could both call on to help. Jealousy didn't have a place in their relationship. Their relationship was strong because they never allowed it in. Instead, they were supportive of other relationships.

A strong relationship is about knowing others are better because of the love and connections they have beyond you. Dad? He had that figured out all along.

# We Value What We Earn

*"You can't just GIVE someone a car."*

Dad lost count of all the people he helped with utility bills over the years. If there were a trophy for "Most Generous Utility Payer," he would have a whole shelf of them. And cars? He's given more cars away than Bob Barker and Pat Sajak combined. Even when he didn't have much to give, he managed to find a way to help.

When I was in early middle school, Dad and I were riding down the road in his pickup truck. We didn't have a lot of money but the people on this street...they were *really* struggling. You could tell just driving through. The front yards looked more like landfills, stray animals had claimed squatters' rights, and windows were held together with duct tape and hope. Sheets tacked up in place of curtains giving the whole place a haunted house but make it a real life kind of vibe. I remember thinking how thankful I was not to live on that street. They did have one perk, every single house backed up to a huge lake. A pretty nice trade-off if you could ignore the rest of the scene.

On this particular day, as we rolled through, Dad spotted the same kid he always saw, fishing at the lake's edge. The boy, who looked to be 16, spent nearly every waking hour with a fishing rod in his hand. The necessity for the boy to feed himself never entered into Dad's mind. As an *avid* fisherman with a love for the sport all he could think was, "*That kid needs a boat.*" When you're passionate about something, you assume everyone else wants to take it to the next level too.

Compelled by his ever-present love for helping others, Dad dropped me off at home and went straight back to visit his new angler-in-training. He handed the boy, Jason, a small piece of paper with our address written in big, bold capital letters, because that's the only way Dad writes anything. He told Jason he had a boat for him. Nothing fancy, just a little Jon boat with a small trolling motor but it would be *his*. There was just one catch (fishing pun *very much* intended).

Jason could come pick up the boat any evening or weekend but he had to bring a parent with him *and* two brand-new life jackets that _he_ purchased. If he did that, Dad would personally deliver the boat to his house, help him unload it, and it would be his. This way he could catch bigger fish in the middle of the lake, the ones hiding in the deeper water.

The parent drop-off was Dad's way of making sure Jason's parents were okay with him having a boat. The life jacket requirement? That was next-level Dad thinking. He easily could have handed over some of the extra life jackets we had lying around but by making Jason buy them himself, Dad knew two things:

1. Jason now had *skin in the game*. He wasn't just getting a free boat; he had to put some of his own resources toward making it safe to use.

2. Because *he* had spent his own money on the life jackets, he was *way* more likely to actually wear them instead of tossing them in a corner and ignoring them like most teenagers do with anything labeled "safety equipment."

That this was one of the first glimpses I got into Dad's philosophy: *We value what we earn.* Little did I know, this lesson was about to extend far beyond fishing boats. Dad did not stop at boat giveaways. He had a whole *fleet* of life lessons on wheels.

Dad learned early on giving people cars was not quite the blessing he thought it was. Sure, they drove off with a new set of wheels but the generosity often found a way of boomeranging back needing a free repair or upgraded version. The original gift usually dented, dirty, or completely broken down and neglected. The interior? A mess. Basic maintenance? A foreign concept. That is IF the car even made it back at all. More often than not, it was abandoned somewhere, left to die a slow, mechanical death because why would someone put money into a car that was free. Either way, before long, he was right back in the same spot, handing over keys to yet another car, only to watch the cycle repeat. It was like a bad sequel to a movie no one wanted to see.

To put a stop to this endless loop, he started applying the same principles he had used in the great boat giveaway: *People take better care of things when they have to invest in them.* Ownership alone was not enough. As he put it, "You can't just GIVE someone a car." There had to be some skin in the game.

He never spelled this out to the person on the receiving end of his generosity. Instead, it became more of a conspiracy between him and his car keys, one where the price of admission was just enough responsibility to make the gift truly matter.

He would find a car that needed new tires to be safe enough to drive, he would take it to get new tires but the new owner would have to pay for the bill. That car needed a new title? Great, they could go ahead and order one themselves and then the car would officially be theirs. The list of these little conditions went on. Each one was just enough to create a sense of responsibility, a way for the recipient to feel like they actually *earned* the car rather than it being handed to them like a freebie at a fair.

He wasn't just giving people cars; he was teaching them the value of taking care of something by making sure they had a hand in making it *theirs*. If they had to work for it, they would cherish it a little more. It was the same lesson he taught Jason with the boat: *a free ride doesn't mean much if you haven't paddled at least part of the way yourself.*

Dad is still the most generous guy you'd meet but now his generosity has a little strategy behind it. He wasn't just handing out keys; he was handing out lessons, lessons in responsibility, ownership, and the simple truth that things mean more when you have invested in them. A little tough love, a few tire bills, and even the cost of a couple of life jackets can make all the difference.

# Mistakes Happen

*"That's why pencils have erasers."*

Statistically speaking, the odds of a fender bender within the first three years of a teenager getting their driver's license are about as high as the odds of them leaving an empty milk carton in the fridge or scattering dirty clothes like modern art across their bedroom floor. I won't say *every* teenager wrecks a car but Brittany and I fit the statistical norm even though we each handled it in our own dramatic fashion.

As the older sibling, I naturally blazed the trail, both on the road and off it. My first accident happened when another driver pulled out in front of me. I swerved, narrowly avoiding catastrophe and gracefully landed at the edge of Mr. Gentry's pumpkin patch. Lucky for me there was a witness who stuck around giving a play-by-play to my parents when they arrived. This kind stranger vouched for my quick reflexes and *impeccable* vehicle control. If there had been a medal for "Heroic Teenage Evasion of Idiotic Driving," I am sure I would have had one hanging on my rearview mirror.

Brittany's first fender bender happened closer to home. She ran a red light and hit another car, which meant her chances of having a kindhearted witness were about as good as her chances of winning the lottery. However, she did have an early arrival on the scene: her boyfriend's Dad. Thanks to living practically within jogging distance, he beat our Dad there by ten minutes, plenty of time to fully embrace his unexpected role as first responder and unofficial accident investigator.

One *might* think his presence would offer some much-needed comfort and reassurance to a panicked teenage girl who had just crunched her first car- a calming voice, maybe a fatherly pat on the shoulder, something in the "Don't worry, kiddo" category. Instead, he showed up like it was the opening arguments at a high-stakes trial and he was determined to get a confession. Poor Brittany barely had time to catch her breath before the questions started flying:

"Where were you looking?"

"How fast were you going?"

"Were you on your phone?"

"Did you even try to brake?"

He even squinted at the car like he was trying to calculate the impact velocity using the angle of the dents.

Perhaps he wasn't *trying* to be mean. Some people just process nervousness and concern in wildly unhelpful ways. He was focused on all the wrong things, determined to uncover every detail of what she *did* or *didn't* do, so he could deliver the grand takeaway message: how *not* to do it again.

Brittany, still in shock and trying to remember if she had even put the car in park, now had the added joy of navigating a surprise roadside deposition while trying not to dissolve into a puddle of tears and regret.

By the time our Dad arrived, the cross-examination was well underway. I'm pretty sure Brittany had already mentally pleaded the Fifth and considered requesting legal representation. To say she was rattled was an understatement. Just the sight of Dad had her eyes filled with tears.

I am certain Dad had no idea what kind of interrogation she had just endured. In fact, I am not sure he even realized how long the other Dad had been on the scene before he arrived. But knowing our Dad, and knowing that he basically knew everyone within a 25-mile radius, it is entirely possible he already had a pretty good read on the situation. Likely, already familiar with this man's "concerned parent" style. He knew warm reassurances like, "*Cars are replaceable but you're not,*" weren't in this guy's emotional toolkit. A torque wrench? Sure. Emotional sensitivity? Only if sarcasm counts.

There they were, our Dad standing just barely over five feet tall, round belly leading the way, like a bowling ball of wisdom and denim. He was usually outfitted in his signature overalls and whether or not he had a shirt on underneath was truly a 50/50 gamble. Sometimes it was a stained T-shirt. Sometimes it was a sunburn. His vibe was pure small-town comfort meets "I'm here to help fix your car or your sink, whatever you need."

The boyfriend's Dad? A sharp contrast in every possible way. He towered over everyone at well over six feet tall, broad-shouldered, perfect posture, and the confident (or cocky) aura of someone who ironed *everything*, including his socks. He usually wore a pressed button-down shirt neatly tucked into slacks or nice jeans. He looked like he might attend a board meeting right after filing an insurance claim.

This unlikely duo, standing side by side on the shoulder of the road, next to Brittany, who looked like she might either cry or drive herself straight into a witness protection program. Our Dad, in true fashion, had sauntered onto the scene with zero urgency but full presence. He didn't need a report or rundown. He took one look at Brittany's tear-filled eyes, wrapped his arm around her shoulder, and said, "That's why pencils have erasers." in the most casual, Dad-of-the-year tone imaginable.

That was it. Just an acknowledgment that, yeah, mistakes happen but they are not the end of the world. They are just part of the process.

Finally, someone with a comforting presence, and, more importantly, *no clipboard of questions.*

Whether you are driving a car, learning how to be an adult, or just trying to make it through your teenage years without too many dings (literal or emotional), the truth is universal: we all mess up. What matters most is what we learn from it and if possible whether we can laugh about it later.

Dad's words, *"That's why pencils have erasers"* were his philosophy, passed down in denim overalls and delivered with the kind of grace that only comes from having seen a lot of life and a fair number of dented bumpers. He understood something that takes most of us years to fully grasp: mistakes are inevitable. The real test isn't whether you avoid every misstep, it's whether you keep going and don't let the fear of failure keep you from getting back behind the wheel, metaphorically or otherwise.

Brittany didn't need a courtroom; she needed compassion. Dad gave it to her, just like he did for me and probably a dozen other kids whose cars and confidence took a hit along the way. We are not defined by our accidents but by how we respond to them. It's one thing to be told that mistakes are part of growing up. It's another to feel it, standing by your wrecked car, heart pounding, eyes blurry with tears, to be met with kindness instead of criticism.

It is true, mistakes happen. Cars get dinged and feelings get bruised. Life is messy but if you are lucky, you have someone to remind you that it's okay to mess up. That's what erasers and second chances are for.

If you are really lucky? You learn to be that person for someone else, too.

# Vulnerability is a Strength

## *"How do you spell..."*

Dad was a worker, the kind of man whose hands told stories before his mouth ever did. Callused, stained with layers of car oil and grease, and almost always sporting a fresh bandage, his hands were a running injury report. If it wasn't from a ball-peen hammer taking a cheap shot, it was from a rogue utility knife or some other self-inflicted wound that came from just trying to survive another day in the life of Joey. He wore his injuries like badges of honor, though you would never catch him admitting he needed stitches.

On weekends and after hours, he was always in his trademark overalls, equal parts utility and fashion statement. During the work week, you could spot him in his transmission shop blues: sturdy jeans and a navy button-down shirt with two pockets, one of which carried an oval patch stitched with his name in a bold white script, "Joey." It looked like it belonged to a man who could rebuild a carburetor in his sleep and he probably could.

He was always tinkering with some type of car or lawnmower but underneath all the grease and grit, he wasn't your stereotypical tough guy. Dad was more of a "truth guy." He didn't talk much about feelings; he didn't have to. His actions did the heavy lifting. He showed the power of letting people in by never pretending to be anything other than exactly who he was.

One of the more personal triumphs of his life was learning to read when I was in kindergarten. These days, he gets by just fine. His reading skills are "good enough" he is never one to read a book but he will flip through the pages to find a section of interest he wants to look at and most people would never guess the adaptive strategies he uses to work through the text. Unless of course you handed him something outside his wheelhouse. If the book wasn't about Bass fishing, duck hunting, or rebuilding transmissions, there was a good chance he was going to squint at it like it just personally offended him. Prior knowledge goes a long way when reading, especially if it's something with a torque converter diagram.

Writing, though, that's another story. It's a lot harder to fake your way through spelling. There's no grease-stained shortcut or trusty shop manual for navigating the endless rules of the English language. They are complex and there are so many that don't follow the conventional patterns, which is why Dad avoided writing like a cat avoids a bath, or like he avoids sushi and anything labeled "diet."

His aversion to writing was deeply rooted but when he became a father, something shifted. Reading had been a mountain he climbed when I started kindergarten but writing, that was personal. In a way, even more important to him because long before I could read or write myself, he was already thinking ahead to something he absolutely *had* to get right: my name.

Like most expecting parents, he and my Mom had picked out two names, one for a boy, one for a girl. The boy's name came easily, no debates, no drama. The girl's name, though? That came straight from the glamorous world of evening soap operas. Mom had fallen head-over-heels for a character's name she heard one night on TV, and she was absolutely sold. If the baby was a girl, that was the name, end of discussion. Dad was fine with it. He liked the name just fine, and even more than that, he liked seeing my Mom light up every time she said it but he had one condition, one non-negotiable.

"You can choose her name," he said, "as long as I get to spell it *my* way. I never want to misspell my own daughter's name."

They agreed and he wrote the spelling of my name for the first time exactly how he could remember it, A-L-I-S-H-A.

It wasn't about grammar or phonics. It was about love and a deep vulnerability that Dad rarely put into words. He didn't spell it the "right" way according to baby name books or spelling conventions. He spelled it the right way for *him* so he would never feel that pang of uncertainty that had followed him through every job application and scribbled note.

For a man who could rebuild a transmission in his sleep but used to sweat over a grocery list, this wasn't just about letters, it was about claiming dignity in a world that sometimes confused book smarts for worth. Even if he couldn't always spell "*transmission*" (yes, he can now, that's one he's committed to memory), he can sure as hell fix one.

His version of writing wasn't shaped by commas or spelling rules but by intention. It's easy to think vulnerability is weakness, especially when your hands are tough and your job is tougher. Choosing to spell my name the way *he* could spell it, he showed what real strength looked like. It came from owning your insecurities, working through them, and still showing up with your heart wide open.

He spelled *Alisha* with all the certainty and love a father could muster, not perfectly but purposefully. Vulnerability isn't weakness, it is the grit behind growth and the heart behind the hard stuff. It's knowing your limits, pushing through them anyway, and still showing up with your whole self, even when your spelling is a little off.

Knowing the story of my name makes me appreciate when I still get to witness his bravery in vulnerable moments. Like when he calls me in the middle of the day to ask how to spell something because he is updating the sign out front of his shop or writing a thank-you message to a customer. I smile every time, knowing how lucky I am that he doesn't feel he has to hide parts of himself from me.

His generosity far outweighs his spelling skills. When he writes a donation check to the school where I serve as Principal, I hand it in to my bookkeeper with immense pride, even if the school's name and the word *elementary* are spelled incorrectly. No one questions it; they don't need to. The intent is always clear.

My absolute favorites are his text messages. Usually short, just enough words to deliver the point until he can call. Every once in a while, he will send a longer one, riddled with spelling errors, autocorrect mishaps, and a few puzzling word choices that require the decoding skills of a former kindergarten teacher. Every time I read one, I feel that same pride I did the day I first heard the story of my name.

These moments are continued reminders of what strength really looks like. The moments that let people see you fully, not just the polished parts but the raw beautiful ones too.

True strength isn't about fixing transmissions or wearing overalls like armor. It's about showing up even with misspellings and oil stains. It's about letting people see you, *especially those you love* the most. It's choosing connection over perfection and asking for help when you need it. It's calling your daughter when you *can't* spell a word because you *trust* her enough to ask. Vulnerability isn't something to be ashamed of, it's the bravest kind of strength. It says, "Here I am. As I am" and there is nothing more powerful than that.

# Struggle Now, Shine Later

*"Just settle down and feel the clutch."*

Learning to drive for my sister and me turned out to be far more than a crash course in keeping a vehicle between two white lines and braking gently enough to avoid launching passengers into the dashboard. It was, in fact, a full-blown *life seminar*, a behind-the-wheel bootcamp in grit, patience, and the valuable lesson that sometimes you just have to take the stairs instead of the elevator. Dad, not exactly a man known for his love of poetry, somehow managed to live his life like Robert Frost's long-lost twin. If there was a difficult road, he wouldn't just take it, he would find a detour that made it even more challenging, just for good measure. When it came time to teach us to drive, *The Road Less Traveled* had a Joey Fuqua rule book of driving courtesies that definitely wasn't included in the driver's ed manual, a manual transmission towing a trailer, and we were expected to merge onto it at full speed.

Driving a manual transmission wasn't just a nice skill to have in Dad's eyes, it was a *non-negotiable life requirement*.

I wasn't going to learn it on some wide, flat, empty stretch of road with birds chirping and sunshine lighting the way. I was going to learn it the Joey Fuqua way: trial by fire and incline.

Once I had the basic idea of how to feather the clutch and gas just enough to keep from stalling out like a rookie, Dad suddenly had a mysterious list of errands that absolutely *had* to be done in his half-ton manual pickup truck and I was his exclusive designated driver.

We live in Tennessee. It is *hilly* in Tennessee. Driving a stick on flat ground is one thing; trying to take off smoothly on a hill is a completely different beast, an angry, gear-grinding, rollback-prone beast. It was terrifying. I would white-knuckle the steering wheel like I was in a NASCAR final, driving Dad to one of his Saturday "errands," silently begging the universe for no one to pull up behind me at a stop sign.

Of course, on one particular afternoon coming back from Nashville, my nightmare scenario unfolded in full cinematic glory. I was approaching *the hill, the* kind of intersection that smells like a burned clutch. The light was red, the slope was steep, and traffic was buzzing around like angry bees. A car pulled up so close behind me I could read the driver's grocery list through their windshield.

"You've got this," he said calmly, like we weren't perched on the edge of a mechanical cliff. In my mind, there was only one logical option: pull the emergency brake, swap places with Dad, and avoid a vehicular manslaughter charge but he was already shaking his head. "Just settle down and *feel* the clutch."

I'm pretty sure I sweat clean through my dress that day. My heart was in my throat, my foot was shaking like a leaf but *somehow*, I did it. I didn't stall. I didn't roll. I didn't ruin anyone's bumper and in that moment Dad's belief in me felt unshakable. Maybe it really was or maybe he just had a lot more faith in clutch mechanics than I did.

Either way, I learned something far more valuable than how to drive stick: that struggle really does have a shine on the other side. Sometimes that shine is just the light turning green, but sometimes, it is realizing you are capable of more than you ever thought.

I already knew how to back up a trailer better than just about anyone in our town, thanks to years of yard work and weekend chores. I was a local legend in reverse. I could back up any trailer with any vehicle... or so I thought.

Then came the next challenge: backing up *that same* half-ton *manual* pickup truck with a trailer hitched to the back. Either surviving hill starts wasn't enough for the teenage me or this was some kind of unofficial Tennessee rite of passage I didn't know about.

As I grumbled that day in protest Dad deadpan as ever said, "Alisha, you never know, someday you might marry someone with a big fancy boat who doesn't know how to back it into the water."

I opened my mouth to argue, then realized I was about to debate hypotheticals with a man who once made me practice backing up a three-foot trailer with a lawnmower dodging dandelions and bumblebees. It was best to say a prayer and plot my path.

I hopped in the truck, rattling down the road with the trailer clunking along behind us like a stubborn mule. We had no real destination, just another "practice run," which in Joey Fuqua terms meant an afternoon at the high school parking lot, navigating tight corners, white lines, and plenty of sloped pavement that would make a seasoned trucker break into a cold sweat.

Luckily there was no audience and there was definitely no air conditioning, just me, Dad, a lot of parking stripes, and one very unforgiving trailer. Every overcorrection, "cut it sharper!" and "use your mirrors!" from Dad in the passenger seat, was adding a new chapter to the Joey Fuqua Driving Handbook.

Little did I know, that book wasn't just about trailers, turn signals, or leaving room for merging traffic. It was about life, about doing the hard things the right way, even when no one's watching. The road less traveled was still calling... and Dad made sure we had the skills to take it. He had an entire chapter dedicated to driving courtesies.

Many of the road courtesies Dad drilled into us during those driving lessons were just considered common sense where we grew up in the South. You always pull over on the shoulder out of respect for a funeral procession. When you passed someone on a backroad, you lifted your left pointer finger in a subtle blend of a wave and a salute, it's a rural Morse code for "I see you, neighbor." You *always* return your shopping cart before getting in your vehicle, regardless of the weather, and if you see an elderly person with theirs, you go get it for them. That was just being raised right.

You never park in someone's yard after it's rained, because ruts are forever. You either go to the car wash or grab a bucket and a rag, because you take pride in what you have. You use your turn signal, even if you are the only one on the road, and if your window is rolled down at a stoplight and so is the person's next to you, you say hello. It's just the friendly thing to do.

Of all the rules in the Joey Fuqua chapter of Driving Courtesies, the one most sacred was this: never use your horn. It's rude. It's aggressive and worst of all, it's lazy. Furthermore, we were to never pull up to someone's house and honk the horn instead of going to the door like a decent human being. If someone did this at our house it was an indicator they were officially not worthy of our company.

That rule sounded simple enough but Brittany had a talent for finding the line and dancing just over it. She is the younger female version of our Dad in most every way.

Shortly after getting her license, she was cruising down the road and happened to pass Dad. Most people would offer the appropriate left-hand salute or maybe an enthusiastic wave. But Brittany? She gave him a cheeky little "toot-toot" of the horn. Not obnoxious or aggressive, just playful.

Dad smiled, waved, and let her roll on... but he was already concocting a plan to remedy the situation. This was a teachable moment wrapped in a minor offense. Fortunately, as someone who worked on vehicles for a living, he had the perfect solution.

A few days later, a very special package arrived at his shop: an old-fashioned, comically loud *Aooga* horn. While Brittany was at school, Dad paid a stealthy visit to her car in the high school parking lot and swapped out her sensible, polite-sounding horn for one that could be heard in the great beyond or at the very least, alert the entire county.

The trap was set.

Not long after, they were out driving together when Dad casually played a card straight out of *her* deck. "Hey, honk at that guy, we know him. He won't recognize me in this car, so just give him a friendly little toot-toot."

Brittany hesitated.

"Yeah," Dad said. "Just a quick little honk."

When she pressed it, it was *game over*. Heads turned. Jaws dropped. Pedestrians startled. And Dad? He had a front row seat to every glorious second. His plan had played out perfectly.

Of course, Brittany couldn't get home fast enough to tell us the story. She had to repeat it three separate times because Dad was laughing so hard he had actual tears streaming down his face and none of us could understand her over the sound of his wheezing cackle.

The horn got a bit more use after that but only in the friendliest of gestures. It became less of a warning device and more of a punchline. Every time she laid on it in the school parking lot at someone's request, people turned to see who was sounding the clown car alarm. She embraced it and most importantly she *never* honked at someone's house, the golden rule of horn honking.

The road less traveled, complete with a manual transmission, a trailer, and the Joey Fuqua Rule Book of Driving Courtesies, taught us far more than how to merge or parallel park. It taught us that grit comes before grace and that just because something's hard doesn't mean it isn't worth doing.

It taught us to *struggle now so we could shine later.*

I didn't marry a man with a fancy boat he couldn't back into the water, like Dad once predicted but I *did* marry a man who loves fancy cars and works hard to afford the things he dreams about. When he bought his first sports car, a Porsche no less, he had it shipped straight to our home. The delivery driver rolled it off the trailer... right into our steep Tennessee driveway. Yes, the Porsche had a manual transmission.

Guess who didn't know how to drive it?

Not that Dad ever needed validation for his methods but he was absolutely and *gloriously* vindicated that day. My husband, bless him, could have chosen an automatic. They were easier to find and more convenient. He wanted the manual because, and I quote, "they're just more fun to drive."

Lucky for him, he married a girl who could not only drive a stick... but could get his dream car out of the driveway while he watched from the passenger seat, sweating just as much as I once did on those hill starts in Nashville traffic.

Turns out, the road less traveled really does make all the difference. If you're lucky, it even comes with a great story and an aooga horn.

# Be Generous but Not Wasteful

*"Any food tastes better eaten out of my fingers."*

Working in the transmission repair business, it wasn't terribly uncommon for Dad to encounter people who needed their vehicles fixed but who didn't have the financial means to pay their repair bill. Over the years, he'd seen it all: jobs traded for repairs, cars sold on the spot, delayed payments that turned into long-lost IOUs, and some downright strange offers in lieu of cash.

When someone proposed an unusual form of payment, he would chuckle, shake his head, and send them politely on their way. After all, you can't exactly pay the electric bill with an autographed Lynyrd Skynyrd guitar or a box of silver flatware (both of which *had* been offered). But every now and then, something would make him pause.

My husband and I had been married just a few years when one of these memorable "I don't have the money but hear me out..." situations rolled into the shop. At first, it seemed like the same old story. But this time, instead of a dusty lawnmower or some tires that didn't fit anything Dad owned, the customer had something a bit shinier up his sleeve.

He offered Dad a *Rolex watch* in trade for the transmission repair he couldn't afford. The irony wasn't lost on Dad. Here was a man who couldn't scrape together enough for a transmission repair, yet was strolling around town wearing a watch that cost more than most people's first car. Dad had been offered a lot of junk in his day but this was a new one.

Things like a Rolex meant absolutely nothing to Dad. Owning a fancy watch was about as practical to him as owning a pet flamingo. Sure, it might turn heads but it wasn't exactly something you needed hanging around every day. There would be very few occasions he would ever wear it and even then Rolex and Louis Vuitton just weren't the kinds of names that got him excited. He knew the brands, could appreciate their value, and even had a few colorful opinions about the people who clamored to own them but they were about as relevant to his world as ballroom dancing shoes at a tractor pull.

The brands Dad personally held in the highest regard? Carhartt, John Deere, and Chevrolet. If it couldn't haul, plow, or survive a grease stain, it just wasn't worth his time.

Nevertheless, Dad decided to play along. He had the man bring the watch in and before sealing the deal he made arrangements to have it authenticated. Dad didn't have a Rolex guy on speed dial but he did have a guy who loved nice things and who kept a foot in the jewelry and watch world purely because it was his hobby. That guy just happened to be my husband, Milt.

Dad figured Milt would either know how to authenticate the watch or would "know a guy" who could. Milt wasn't about to let the weight of a potential fake Rolex sit squarely on his conscience. He took the watch to be professionally authenticated. It checked out, everything was real. Genuine Rolex movement, paperwork, box, everything was legit from crown to clasp.

Dad took the deal.

The man got a new transmission and Dad walked away the owner of a Rolex, a shiny hunk of expensive metal with numbers so tiny he couldn't see them well enough to tell the time. It didn't matter anyway because he found out if he wasn't going to wear it every day he needed a special winding box just to keep it running. Otherwise, every time he pulled it out, he'd have to set the time all over again, which, in his opinion, was entirely too much drama just to figure out if it was almost time to watch Andy Griffith.

Milt was practically bouncing with excitement. He immediately started shopping for watch winders, explaining the fine points of automatic movements, the prestige of the model, and the "investment value" of the piece, as if Dad had just accidentally stumbled into the Secret Society of the Ultra Classy.

After patiently listening to Milt's full presentation on what made this particular Rolex so special, how to care for it, and why it was an asset worth treasuring, Dad finally looked at him, grinned, and said, "You know, I think it would be best if you just go ahead and serve as the manager of this thing for me. You hold on to it, wear it, take care of it, and make sure it gets whatever it needs. That way, if I ever need to wear it, I'll know where to find it."

Milt didn't see it coming and neither did I. Dad had planned to give Milt the watch all along. The empty box and paperwork to the watch came wrapped under the Christmas tree making the gift official a couple years later. Generosity was something Dad modeled constantly, in his own unmistakable way.

He knew how much Milt loved watches and jewelry, the craftsmanship, the history, the little mechanical miracles ticking away on a wrist. Dad also knew that Milt had never owned a Rolex and probably wouldn't for quite some time. This wasn't just a casual handoff of something shiny; it was Dad's way of giving Milt something that was worth more than just its market value. It carried meaning.

It was a gift from a father-in-law to a son-in-law, sure, but the bond it represented went deeper than that. It connected them in a new way. It was Dad's way of saying, *I see you. I see how different you are from me and I appreciate it. I respect it.*

Several years later, Milt, proudly sporting his Rolex, found himself at Mom and Dad's house, where, somehow, the conversation between him and Dad took an unexpected culinary turn:
Spam.
The canned meat. The pride of the pantry in hard times.

Dad was explaining in detail how good Spam could be when it was fried up in a hot skillet, crispy edges, sizzling in its own magical mystery grease. Milt, on the other hand, was deeply skeptical. With his eyebrows cocked, he was eyeing Dad with the same expression you might reserve for someone insisting that gas station sushi was a hidden delicacy.

Eventually, Milt suggested they open a can and fry some up so he could try it for himself. Normally, Dad would jump at the opportunity to cook something and have you taste it often bypassing utensils altogether, proudly declaring, "Any food tastes better eaten out of my fingers." But this time, he didn't move. He had a few cans tucked away in the pantry but he wasn't about to waste a perfectly good can of Spam on a man who had already decided it looked like something scraped off a science lab floor.

Milt pressed him a little more, even offering to buy him a brand-new can to replace the one they opened. He promised he'd give it a fair shot but Dad still didn't budge. He didn't believe Milt's mind was open enough to give Spam a real chance and he wasn't about to sacrifice good food to prove a point.

At our house, being wasteful had more to do with intention than frugality. It was about being mindful of what you truly needed or genuinely valued. Whether it was a can of Spam or a Rolex, the same principle applied: you didn't waste good things on empty gestures. You gave meaningfully and you held onto the things that still had a purpose.

Dad had no problem being generous, he often was but generosity had to have a purpose. It had to be real. He would gladly hand over a Rolex if he thought it would be worn and loved but crack open a can of Spam just to watch someone wrinkle their nose and push it around a plate?

Not a chance.

Milt didn't get to taste Spam that day and that was exactly how Dad wanted it. To him some things like a good can of Spam and a well-placed lesson weren't meant to be wasted on a half-hearted audience.

In Dad's world, you didn't waste what was valuable. You placed it carefully into the hands of someone who would truly appreciate it, care for it, and when the time came you would pass it along with the same intention.

A Rolex and a can of Spam— unlikely teachers of a simple, lasting truth. Be generous but never wasteful. Give fully when it matters and hold onto what still has good left to give.

# Always Stop to Enjoy the Music

*"I definitely could have been a rock star if I would have ever picked up a guitar."*

We believed in working hard and giving everything we did our full attention, even if that meant folding laundry like it was an Olympic sport. Still, amid all the hustle, Dad had a unique gift: he never forgot to stop and enjoy the music.

He wasn't musically gifted but that never stood in the way of his confidence. "I definitely could have been a rockstar if I'd ever picked up a guitar," he'd say, with a grin that suggested he actually believed it.

*Dad on the mic, introducing the band in our backyard—
secretly wishing he were the one playing lead guitar.*

Despite his lack of natural talent or formal training, Dad loved music. Not in a casual, "I like to listen to the radio in the car" kind of way. This was a full-blown, soul-level relationship with music. It was the mantra he lived by: never be too busy to stop and enjoy the music and he modeled it in the most unexpected and inconvenient ways.

For example, Dad built a garage next to our house. When I say garage, I mean *Garage*, with a capital G. It cast a bit of a shadow on our actual house. It was taller, the brick was newer, and it even had fancy crown molding inside Dad salvaged from a friend's job site.

The garage was built for practical things: vehicle storage, tool tinkering, and a space for Dad to work on cars without crawling around in the driveway. However, one of the very first things installed wasn't a workbench or even shelves. It was a sound system.

He mounted speakers high in the corners like sentries guarding the kingdom of good tunes. There was a control box set up so he could switch between his favorite CDs with a remote, which he wielded like a conductor's baton. The garage quickly became a concert venue, a music sanctuary, and sometimes a place where he tinkered on a car or two.

If Dad was in the garage with the bay door open and the music playing, you were getting a show. He would call you over and make you stand there while he queued up Peter Frampton's "Do You Feel Like I Do" from the live album-thirteen minutes and forty-five seconds of guitar virtuosity.

He knew every bent note and feedback squeal. He performed it. He felt it on a cellular level. It was a performance that demanded an audience.

"Hold on, wait 'till you hear this next part," he'd shout over the music if he'd catch you trying to inch away.

You weren't just listening to music. You were witnessing a moment. Music wasn't background noise, it was the main event for Dad and he made sure that, no matter how busy life got, we took time to press pause on life and enjoy the soundtrack.

When music showed up in our lives, sometimes unexpectedly. Dad never missed a chance to stop and take it in. These surprise encounters were just as important as the planned stereo concerts in the garage.

One evening, Dad and I were leaving a church class together. Just the two of us. The parking lot was nearly empty, dimly lit by flickering street lamps, and a heavy fog had settled over everything, giving the night a mystical, almost movie-like atmosphere. We strolled slowly toward his truck, chatting about the class and what we needed to get done once we got home. Just everyday stuff.

From somewhere beyond the tree line near the church, a sound drifted through the fog, soft at first, but unmistakable- bagpipes. Someone was playing bagpipes.

We both stopped silently confirming we were indeed hearing the same thing. Whatever we had been talking about was completely forgotten. The bagpipes had taken over.

We walked slowly toward the truck, the haunting melody echoed through the mist and neither of us made a move to get inside. Dad didn't say a word. I knew we weren't going anywhere. I didn't want to.

We stood in an empty church parking lot, surrounded by fog listening to some mystery musician play slow, soul-stirring tunes on their bagpipes, just us and the music.

It felt more spiritual than the class we had just left.

I heard bagpipes again a few days later as I walked into the garage. Dad was listening to an instrumental version of "Amazing Grace," a new CD to his multi-disc changer. Peter Frampton occasionally had to take a back seat to the stirring sounds of a highland melody.

Sometimes, slowing down and enjoying the music just finds *you*. It could be an epic guitar solo echoing through the garage, Jerry Lee Lewis effortlessly "tickling the keys" on the stereo, or an impromptu fog-filled bagpipe concert in an empty church parking lot, slowing down to enjoy music was a sacred ritual Dad believed in.

Music is a portal. A way to reset and let the chaos of life fall away.

If a good song came on the radio just as Dad pulled into the driveway, he wouldn't rush. He would shift the truck into park, lean his head back against the seat, and let the engine hum quietly as the music took over. With the volume turned up as loud as necessary to block out the rest of the world, he'd sit and let the music wash over him.

He would eventually wander into the kitchen, humming or singing a few of his favorite lines, a relaxed grin on his face. The tension of the day was gone. The to-do list forgotten. In its place was a man ready to enjoy the simple gift of being with family and friends. Music was how he made that shift in small intentional moments of pause.

Friday and Saturday nights, or any vacation day, were especially suited for these musical interludes. Some people, those with actual musical talent, sit on their back porch, strumming a guitar and singing in harmony with the crickets. Others, apparently, play bagpipes for unwitting audiences in church parking lots.

But Dad? He believed back porches were best used for firing up a speaker and blasting his latest curated playlist from his favorite music streaming service. (That subscription, by the way, was the most successful Father's Day gift we ever gave him.)

No matter how busy life gets, how long the to-do list becomes, or how loud the world becomes, there's always room to stop, just for a moment, and let the music in.

Whether it's a classic rock solo echoing a garage that smells faintly of motor oil, or a haunting bagpipe melody drifting through the night, these moments matter. They connect us. They remind us that life is about more than just going through the motions, it is about feeling things deeply.

Turn up the volume, pause for the chorus, and remember: you're never too busy to stop and enjoy the music.

# Give Purposefully

*"You wanna go for a ride?"*

Gift-giving was something Dad did in his own way. His gifts were often unusual and sometimes unexpected, never tied with bows and perfectly matched paper. They came with a dash of practicality and a sense of timing that made them unforgettable. If he had something he wasn't using and knew someone who could enjoy it more, he didn't hesitate, he would pass it along no fuss, just, "Here. You'll get more use out of it than I will."

A few years into owning their lake house, Dad did just that.

There was a guy named Kevin who lived nearby and looked after Mom and Dad's "toys," boats, jet skis, and all the fun stuff that came with lake life. Kevin was the kind of guy Dad could count on if he needed him. He kept the boats spotless, winterized them with care, then brought them back to life each spring like some sort of outboard motor whisperer. When something broke, Dad didn't ask how much it would cost, he just called Kevin. He trusted the job would be done right and for a fair price.

When Kevin and his young boys asked to borrow our jet ski, Dad didn't hesitate. Every time they brought it back, Kevin would light up telling stories about how much fun they'd had out on the water. His boys loved it, and their joy was contagious.

Eventually, it became obvious that Kevin and his kids were getting way more use, and way more fun, out of the jet ski than we were. Dad was using it just often enough to keep the battery alive. Kevin kept it running, handled repairs, covered it, uncovered it, and basically treated it like his own... Dad made it official.

He gave it to him.

Selling it would have made a few bucks but giving it away brought a kind of profit that couldn't be measured in dollars. The joy of watching someone enjoy something he didn't need? That was worth more than any price tag. There was always more reward in giving than receiving.

Sometimes Dad's gifts were just like that, spontaneous and rooted in joy. He loved seeing other people light up, especially when they had worked hard and shown gumption. You had to have hustle. Dad didn't hand things out for free but he would happily bless someone who had shown effort and a good attitude.

Other times, his gifts met deeper needs. He had a particular sensitivity when it came to helping people who were struggling. He understood how pride and dignity often walked hand in hand.  When someone was having a hard time making ends meet, he didn't show up at the door with a check or an envelope. He showed up at the utility department. Light bills and water bills were paid directly at the source. When the bill arrived in the mail, it simply read: Paid in Full.

That was all the conversation Dad needed.

Two people smiled that day, one with relief, the other with the joy of knowing they had helped make life a little easier. Dad believed in giving with humility and helping without fanfare.

The soft resolve with which Dad preferred to give, especially when meeting a real need, wasn't always possible. As much as he loved helping behind the scenes, not every situation allowed for silent generosity. Sometimes, the need was too public. Sometimes, the solution couldn't be privately paid in advance or slipped in an envelope. Sometimes, helping someone meant stepping right into the middle of their struggle.

Like the time Sal, the boat dock attendant, needed to have all his teeth pulled.

This was a guy who worked hard in his own way. He greeted every lake-goer with a friendly nod, tied off boats like a pro, and even when complaining about the heat, the splinters, or the endless stream of weekend chaos he made light of it, inevitably making those listening laugh. He didn't ask for much and certainly wasn't one to seek attention. When word got around that he had to have all his teeth removed and couldn't afford dentures afterward, it was the kind of news that stuck with Dad.

This was about a man's ability to eat; to carry on a conversation without self-consciousness. This was about dignity and he couldn't stand someone being denied their dignity.

Dentures weren't a bill he could sneak in and pay at the window. There was no way to do this anonymously or from the sidelines. So, he did the only thing he knew to do: he stepped in and offered to cover the cost.

Dad understood something a lot of people miss: real generosity sometimes means being present. It means standing beside them in a vulnerable moment, and saying, "I've got you."

A few years later, Sal, the same boat dock attendant, now sporting a full set of teeth and a face even more weathered by the sun, was still holding things down at the lake. His skin had taken on that signature leathery look that only comes from decades of working under a southern summer sun, and his smile, finally whole, was still subtle yet had a certain sparkle to it.

Sal had become something of a legend around the marina. He knew every boater by name and every creak in the dock boards by sound alone. While his job wasn't exactly a get-rich-quick scheme, unless "rich" meant in boat and fishing stories, it was clear he was doing what he loved.

The only thing missing? A working boat of his own.

He once had owned a modest boat that sputtered along just fine, until it didn't. Eventually, the repairs outpaced the ride and the vessel was pronounced officially unseaworthy. Still, Sal didn't complain about it or try to coerce someone into buying him a new one. He just adapted. He'd soak up the peace of the water from the dock or the occasional "Hey Sal, you wanna go for a ride?" from grateful boat owners whose crafts he kept running smoother than a catfish slipping through lake water.

Dad noticed.

He saw how Sal's face lit up when he was out on the water. He noticed how he never asked for anything, yet gave so much of himself to keep the marina humming in his own way. When Dad came across the opportunity to buy a small boat, nothing flashy, but just right, he didn't hesitate.

He bought the boat, cleaned it up, and handed Sal the keys with a smile that might have been wider than Sal's, even with the full denture advantage. The reward was never in the thing itself; it was in the giving. Watching Sal's jaw drop, followed by a grin so big it probably caused a breeze, was more than worth it.

Sal had a passion and purpose even without a boat. Now he also had the wind in his face and the freedom to chase the sunset all the way down Kentucky Lake on his own terms.

Dad gave because he believed people deserved to feel supported and set free to do what they loved. It didn't matter if he was paying a bill in secret, gifting a jet ski just for fun, or putting a boat in the hands of a man who found peace on the water, his generosity always came with purpose.

True giving is about knowing someone well enough to see what they need and caring enough to meet that need without expecting anything in return.

The most meaningful gifts aren't wrapped with ribbons or followed by speeches. They are wrapped in thoughtfulness and purpose.

Giving, when done with heart, has the power to restore dignity and remind people that they matter, even if all you are giving is a boat, a break, or a moment of belief.

# The Gift of Predictability

What do you get the person who's impossible to shop for at Christmas?

The gift of predictability, a memory lovingly anchored to a certain thing, or in our case, to a place.

For my sister Brittany and me, by the time we were grown, the thrill of unwrapping our own Christmas presents had faded. When we gathered as a family, it wasn't about what was under the tree for us anymore. The real magic was watching our kids dive headfirst into piles of presents like tiny, sugar-fueled tornadoes, squealing with delight over whatever trendy chaos had been scribbled on their wish lists that year.

Not long after we had both had children Brittany and I made a mom-level decree that would've shocked our pre-kid selves: no more adult gift-giving within our little family circle. We announced it like two wise matriarchs bestowing peace upon the land. No more hunting for novelty socks or panicking over which candle scent screams "pleasant but not migraine-inducing." We didn't need more "stuff," and we didn't want it either. Simpler was better. The focus would be on the kids and keeping both our holiday budgets and blood pressure at manageable levels.

Of course, we still gave a little something to Mom and Dad, typically a framed photo of the grandkids or on years when we managed to coordinate schedules and matching outfits a professionally shot family portrait printed on canvas. In return, they stuck to a sweet, predictable tradition of their own: giving each of us (and our husbands) a hand painted Christmas tree ornament with a couple hundred dollars discreetly (or not-so-discreetly) tucked inside. It was our agreement, our family rhythm. Everyone knew the drill.

Except Dad.

Dad has always marched to the beat of his own off-brand, slightly-off-key Christmas drum. Every year he would head out on a last-minute shopping spree. His destination? Always the same: Walgreens. Home of "as seen on TV" items and the inexplicably grandiose beauty aisle that smells like a mix of rosewater and sunscreen. While the rest of us relaxed with cocoa, our shopping done, Dad was still wandering the aisles of a drugstore, armed with little more than some loosely held notions and the guidance of a sweet unsuspecting lady at the beauty counter.

He would return with bags filled with an eclectic assortment of lotions, bath bombs, lip balms, and the occasional rogue massager. The pièce de résistance? A bottle of perfume he personally selected for each of us, usually based on whatever had the prettiest bottle and whichever glowing review the beauty clerk gave about its scent or the celebrity behind it.

This became his tradition.

Dad's contribution to the holiday chaos, wrapped in whatever paper he could find, sealed with love, and possibly a BOGO sticker. No amount of protest, budgeting logic, or heartfelt "we don't need anything" speeches could sway him. He was a man on a mission and not even the Ghost of Christmas Practicality could stop him.

We still laugh, sometimes lovingly, sometimes incredulously, at Dad's stubborn insistence on breaking the "no gifts for adults" rule. Over time, those bags of Walgreens treasures, hand-selected with more heart than strategy, became something we all secretly looked forward to. We would joke about who got the sparkiest lip gloss or the strongest-smelling perfume, and we would roll our eyes in humor as we unwrapped yet another lavender-scented foot soak. Beneath the laughter was something deeper: a sense of warmth, of being known and remembered in the way only a Dad who never read a label but always showed up could provide.

In a season so often filled with busyness and Pinterest-level pressure, his quirky, dependable little tradition became an anchor. A small and humorously predictable act of love. We didn't need the gifts but we came to treasure the ritual. Predictability, as it turns out, is its own kind of magic. It gives us something to count on and something to smile about before it even happens. It turns the ordinary into the unforgettable.

Each Christmas, we came to expect a gift bag of slightly mismatched self-care items and a perfume bottle bedazzled with rhinestones or Burberry Plaid. More than that we came to cherish the joy of knowing he would never stop trying to surprise us with something we didn't need, wrapped in the unwavering love we always did.

That's the gift of predictability, the kind of love that shows up year after year, sometimes even in a Walgreens bag.

# Pride Without the Spotlight

*"Most parents are lucky if they get one kid who turns out good. I got two."*

There comes a moment in every family when the shift inevitably happens: the torch of hosting gets passed from the parents to the children. No formal ceremony, just one holiday after another, transitioning to a new location, and a new generation. In our family, that shift began just a few years after I got married. First, it was Christmas, then Thanksgiving, followed by birthdays and other big family milestones.

It felt a bit strange. Mom and Dad had always been the ones to open their home and orchestrate the beautiful chaos of a holiday meal but life moved forward. Brittany and I had families of our own and with growing households came the practical need for more space. Our modest childhood home, where we learned to walk and decorated the refrigerator with our art projects, just couldn't contain all of us anymore, unless the weather cooperated and we could spill out onto the back porch. The larger family

117

gatherings began to rotate to our homes where we became the hosts.

Mom and Dad visited our homes regularly but there was something about the larger family events with all the kids running around, extended family all competing to get a word in, and the smells of roasting turkey and homemade bread wafting through the air that seemed to stir something deeper in Dad. It was subtle, but unmistakable: a glisten in his eyes and his chest held just a little higher. His pride simply smiled and soaked in the moment.

Pride.

Not the boastful kind. The kind that wells up in a parent who sees the seeds they planted bloom into something beautiful.

Growing up, our parents never sat us down and said, "We want you to have more than we did." It's clear that's exactly what they hoped for. They had worked hard to provide for us. Holidays were magical, yes, but they were also expensive and exhausting for them. It brought them joy to see us take the reins. It meant their sacrifices had yielded something: stability, success, traditions passed on, and two daughters who are a team who genuinely enjoy each other's company. The legacy they built was thriving.

Dad never walked into our houses for a family gathering or otherwise empty-handed. He never arrived just as a guest.

I'm not talking about the dish they were bringing to contribute to the meal; that was expected. I'm talking about *something extra*. Something just for us. He never called it a hostess gift but that is exactly what it was.

They would burst through the door simultaneously, sometimes one through the back door, one through the front, but always somehow in sync, like they had coordinated the moment for theatrical flair. Mom carried the obligatory cobbler or pot of turnip greens and was quick to set everything down. Dad would trail behind her, his arms full of his signature surprise haul: a produce box brimming with fresh peaches or homegrown tomatoes. A box from the butcher shop with fresh ground sausage and pork chops he had carefully sealed in airtight FoodSaver bags and labeled with the date only in his unmistakable handwriting using a black Sharpie. The man could not resist bringing gifts.

His entrance was always a bit of an event. The front door would fly open like a gust of wind and it was as if a tiny tornado had just blown in. The box of goods thudded onto the kitchen island. His coat would usually get dropped somewhere between the foyer and the piano bench. He would greet us with a one-armed hug in passing, already halfway to the floor to greet the family dog like it had been years instead of days. The rhythm of it all was so consistent, it might as well have been choreographed.

Once the produce was unpacked and order had been restored, he'd begin his monologue, part roadside produce stand review and part proud Dad commentary: "These peaches? Sweetest I've found anywhere." "Those tomatoes, one bite of them and you'll know they didn't come from the *grocery store*. They taste like they are straight off the vine"

"This pork? Fresh as it gets. That hog was still walking around *yesterday morning*."

We always "ooh" and "ahh" as if it is our first time hearing it, even though we have come to expect both the treats and the enthusiastic sales pitch. We don't mind. It is not really about the food. It is his way of giving. His way of *providing*. Just a man who showed his love in practical ways letting his pride ride in a produce box.

The moment I cherish most usually comes just before they leave. Amid the gathering of Tupperware and goodbyes, Dad would pull me, or Brittany, or both of us, into a final hug. His voice would drop just a little softer and shakier than usual and he would say, "I'm just so proud of you." Sometimes he adds, "You know, most parents are lucky if they get *one* kid who turns out good. I got two."

That line always makes me smile. Perhaps part joke but if you know Dad, you know he means every word. What he is really saying is: *You have made a life for yourself. A good one.*

What more could any of us want than that?

The greatest gift a parent can give is belief. The steady kind. The kind that shows up with a box of peaches and pork chops, a knowing smile, and a hug that says, "You're doing it and I'm proud."

Love doesn't always come wrapped in grand gestures or dramatic speeches. Sometimes it comes through casseroles and butcher boxes, through faithful presence and small rituals repeated year after year. It is found in the act of showing up, faithfully, consistently, and in leaving just enough space for your children to grow into something even greater than you imagined.

# Celebrate with Humility

*"Did you call her?"*

Our parents weren't the type to brag to their friends about their children's accomplishments. They felt excessive adult bragging wasn't necessary. They weren't the type of parents who *must* just show you just one more blurry photo of their kids' first spaghetti dinner.

They weren't showy about their pride. They didn't need to be. Their love and support were woven into the fabric of our lives, always felt even when not loudly spoken. While some parents metaphorically carried a bullhorn around to boast about their children, ours taught us something deeper: humility doesn't minimize success, it creates space for it to be received with grace. Like any proud parents they got excited about our achievements. They sent out graduation announcements and called relatives with particularly big news.

They were never the kind to flood conversations with, "Did you hear what my kid did?" or make sure every single dinner party turned into a PowerPoint presentation on Brittany and me.

They wanted us to understand the power of letting our achievements speak for themselves.

Dad especially held back. Even when someone would approach him in town, maybe a parent whose child I had taught, or someone whose kid finally learned to swim thanks to Brittany, he wouldn't launch into a soliloquy about how great his daughters were. This may have been the only time in his life when Dad became more of a listener than a talker. Usually, he couldn't resist tossing in a story, a joke, or at least an opinion (solicited or not) but when someone started complimenting us? He just stood there silently grinning like he had won the lottery. He felt he had won the parenting lottery so this took tremendous restraint.

It was one of the rare times he put his words away and let the moment speak for itself. He had plenty to say but he chose silence allowing the voices and perspective of others to fill the space. He didn't want to dilute their kind words with anything that might come across as arrogant or boastful. Sometimes the best way to honor a compliment is simply to receive it with reverence. It wasn't about false humility; it was about letting others reflect back what he already knew in his heart.

In those moments, his silence was a form of celebration, proof that humility doesn't shrink from pride. It just gives it more depth.

The second he got the chance he would tell us about it. He'd recount the entire encounter: where it happened (usually the gas station or grocery store but occasionally even on a test drive) and he shared every detail including how it made him feel. It was like his own private trophy moment and we were the lucky ones who got to see him lift the cup. These were the celebrations where humility allowed him to keep close to savor instead of perform.

Because he owned a business in the small town where we grew up, moments like these found him more often than they did Mom. Whether he was grabbing a gallon of milk, stopping by the fruit stand, or chatting with someone in the meat department, he couldn't go many places without someone recognizing him and knowing his connection to us. If someone shared a story or offered congratulations, his pride would rise just beneath the surface.

That was his way respectful and yet fully present in the moment. True humility doesn't hide joy; it simply makes room for others to feel it too.

He didn't grab a bullhorn and stand in the town square when Brittany became licensed as a biology teacher and then as if that wasn't impressive enough finished her second degree and became a registered nurse. He didn't go around telling everyone I had defended my dissertation and earned a doctorate. If someone mentioned it to him? If they had seen it on social media or heard it through the grapevine? He would smile that familiar smile and let them speak every word they wanted to say. He never interrupted. Just nodded, soaking it all in, as proud as a man could be without making it all about himself.

He was a master of letting pride live quietly. He understood when pride was filtered through humility it became more magnetic rather than off-putting. To him pride didn't need to be announced to be real. He felt it deeply, he didn't need to say a word.

But humility doesn't mean invisibility. It means timing. For Dad, the time eventually came and when it did anyone within a 25-mile radius and access to a telephone knew it.

At some point, the quiet, behind-the-scenes kind of pride gave way to something a little less subtle. Dad didn't suddenly start handing out printed résumés of our accomplishments at the gas station- but the same man who once nodded humbly when people praised his daughters had suddenly become unapologetically more proactive.

When I was named a finalist for our State Principal of the Year it was a big deal to *me* but to Dad? It was *the* deal. His own personal Oscars moment. There was no whispering the news. He *broadcasted* it.

He called everyone and I do mean *everyone*. I owe half my hometown an apology for whatever appointment or grocery run Dad unknowingly delayed while he stood in the middle of their day, beaming with pride and *talking at full volume* about the award. The man even used his limited texting abilities to forward news articles about it. I honestly didn't know he could send links. He barely knew how to *open* them. But for this? He leveled up.

It was as if years of keeping it all tucked in had finally bubbled over, and now? He was *unleashed*.

This was no longer the Dad who smiled silently while others sang our praises. This was the newly self-appointed spokesperson for "My Daughters Are Amazing, Inc." and business was booming.

One of my favorite examples, though I can only laugh about it now, came from a high school friend of mine, Craig. We had lost touch since graduation but there was an unspoken understanding: if either of us ever needed something, the other would be there.

When his name popped up on my phone one evening my heart sank just a little. Isn't it awful how our brains go straight to worst-case scenarios? I answered with an overly cheerful, way-too-high-pitched hello...bracing myself for bad news while pretending not to.

"Hey Craig, how lucky am I to hear from you!"

We exchanged the usual pleasantries before he cut to the chase.

"I just wanted to say congratulations. Finalist for State Principal of the Year? That's amazing."

I rolled my eyes, chuckled, thanked him, and tried to shift the conversation elsewhere. Then, he revealed the real reason for his call.

Apparently, *my Dad*, the same man who spent my entire life downplaying our success in public, choosing humility over hype, drove to Craig's house just to tell him the news *in person*. Not only that, he instructed Craig to call me about it. When Craig didn't call right away? Dad followed up. *Repeatedly.*

Every time he saw Craig afterward, he would ask, "Hey, did you call Alisha yet? Did you tell her congratulations? I am just so proud of her man."

It was like a grassroots campaign of fatherly pride and my Dad was out knocking doors.

Because he had spent a lifetime practicing humility, his celebration didn't feel forced, it felt earned. His joy wasn't met with eye-rolls but with warmth, because he had built the credibility to cheer loudly.

It would have been easy to shake my head at Dad's sudden transformation from quiet supporter to full-blown street team captain and trust me, I did more than once. Underneath the awkward texts, the repeated storytelling, and the surprise phone calls he prompted on my behalf, something really beautiful was unfolding.

He was celebrating what this award represented to him: years of watching his daughters become the kind of women he had always hoped we'd grow up to be. The man who had spent decades listening with a smile had simply reached a point where the smile wasn't enough anymore. He was getting a bullhorn.

That's the thing about pride rooted in love and humility. It may begin with nods and knowing glances but eventually it finds its voice. When it does it sounds a lot like gratitude. Gratitude for the journey, for the outcomes, and for the chance to finally say out loud: "Look at my girls. Would you just look at them?"

Humility doesn't mean you can't celebrate. Sometimes, it means you absolutely should.

# Stay Grounded

As much as you want the people you love to soar, to find success that eclipses anything you have ever done, there's still a hope nestled in your heart: that they'll stay grounded while they fly. That no matter how high they climb, they will keep their feet firmly planted in who they are and where they came from.

Dad had a way of making sure we never forgot that. He did not go about it in any traditional Instagram-worthy fashion. His methods were a bit more rustic. Unfiltered. Occasionally metallic and always memorable.

Whenever our families would gather for birthdays or any holiday that gave us the excuse to eat too much and gather together, Dad would roll in like a one-man reminder that status and success should never outweigh character and connection. Our houses might have become more extravagant and our closets filled with clothes that actually required dry cleaning but none of that fazed him. He showed up exactly how he wanted: overalls or worn in jeans that had seen better decades, a stained t-shirt, and a tattered box of something from a local farm, fresh vegetables, fruit, or a suspiciously large quantity of pork chops or sausage.

Standing in cheerful defiance, the gift table exploded with color-coordinated wrapping paper and bows and gift bags bursting with toys or tech accessories. Then here comes Dad, whom our kids affectionately call "Boss," pulling silver Coors Light beer cans out of his tattered box. No bow. No wrapping paper. Just a cold one. At least, that is what it looked like on the outside.

Coors Light is *Dad's* beer of choice but not just any Coors Light the kind that came in the special wide-mouth aluminum cans with the screw-on tops. Coors couldn't have made a product more suited to him if they'd called him up to ask.

Not only were they harder for a toddler to sip from accidentally but the mouth was larger than a quarter and smaller than a half dollar, *perfect* for what he had in mind.

Dad was simple in every way and nowhere was that simplicity more pronounced than in his stubborn resistance to electronic anything, especially electronic money. He didn't trust it. He barely tolerated credit cards. Never mind PayPal or crypto. He paid for everything in folding cash. If cash wouldn't work, he would mail you a check. This way of living meant he accumulated a decent amount of change in his pockets. That change added up.

Enter the Beer Can Bank.

Each of these specially chosen Coors Light cans was cleaned out, filled to the brim with coins then sealed back up. Then came the final touch. Using a thick black Sharpie, he'd scrawl a child's name on the can. One can for Addison.

One for Caroline. One for Rhett. *Personalized and mildly questionable if spotted by a neighbor.*

I'll never forget the first time he passed out these special beer-can gifts. He walked in, placed the cans silently on the counter like it was the most natural thing in the world, and said, "Brought the kids something." There sat a trio of labeled Coors Light cans sitting on the kitchen island, suspiciously heavy and undeniably intriguing.

The looks on our kids' faces were confused and horrified. These are kids who'd grown up differently than Brittany and I did. They didn't split wood to keep warm. They had never weeded a garden in July and they certainly didn't know how to stripe a lawn with a lawnmower. They knew trampoline parks, app stores, sushi nights, and the magic of two-day shipping. They had no idea how much fun could be had during a firewood-stacking contest, sinking in the mud up to your knees after a good rain in the garden, or how soothing the rattle of a lawnmower can be on a nice day.

When presented with what looked like a cold beer as a gift from their granddad, they didn't quite know what to do but curiosity won. One of them picked it up, clearly surprised by the weight, and twisted off the lid.

Out poured a cascade of coins the kind that adds up to real money fast. Their eyes lit up like they had discovered One-Eyed Willy's treasure. Within minutes, all three cans had been cracked open, coins counted and sorted, and plans made for how to spend it. It was a fortune to them but also in meaning. It felt like magic. It was Boss's magic and it came in a beer can.

*Dad's Coors Light Beer Can Banks for each of the kids.*

The real gift was the moment. A joke wrapped in sincerity. A gesture that said: "Don't ever forget where you come from. That was the deeper lesson. Dad gave gifts that were functional and totally unexpected. The cans were full of coins and filled with value.

It was also his way of reminding Brittany and me, and now our children, value doesn't come dressed in designer packaging. You don't need a shiny bow to be important. The most meaningful things can come in the humblest containers. Staying grounded means understanding that flash doesn't equal substance and what matters most will always be what is inside.

Our kids may have laughed about their "beer gifts" at first. But one day, when life has piled on just a little too much, they'll remember those silver cans, the clink of coins that spilled out, and the man who gave them.

They'll remember that the goal in life isn't just to rise, it's to rise while staying rooted. Just like Boss taught us.

The Coors Light cans left a lasting impression because of what they represented; what they held was irrelevant. They are Boss's reminder, wrapped in aluminum and Sharpie, that no matter what kind of zip code you live in, what kind of car you drive, or what name is stitched into your clothing label, you are never better than anyone else.

He showed it in every unwrapped gift and handful of change collected with patience and purpose. Real value is found in the way you treat people and how well you remember your roots. Success is hollow if it makes you forget where you started or who helped you along the way.

Dad knew that character isn't thinking less of yourself, it's thinking of yourself less. That kind of grounding is something you can't buy, no matter how many coins you cram into a beer can. It has to be lived and passed down through generations in how you show up for others and how you give.

When I think about what I want for my daughter, Addison, not just now but long after we're gone, it's not that she has the biggest house or the most impressive title. It's that she grows up to be kind and rooted in something deeper than appearance or status. I hope she remembers the man who showed up with vegetables in a box and coins in a can and the way he made everyone in the room feel seen and loved.

Even the tallest trees draw their strength from the roots you can't see.

# Choose What's Right Over What's Easy

*"Our family has always done the right thing; this is one of those times."*

There are moments in life when you absolutely *know* what the right thing is but instead of charging toward it with clarity before your brain could object you find yourself inching along the edge of it toeing the line. That was my sister and me over a funeral.

This was for someone we had once been close with, someone who had shared holidays with us, laughed around our dinner table, and knew our family well enough to use the good towels in the guest bathroom without asking. Somewhere along the way, they quit showing up and returning calls. Eventually, it was clear: we had been written out. Not just of one person's life, but seemingly out of their whole family tree.

If you have ever been estranged from someone you care about without knowing *why*, you'll understand the emotional gymnastics involved. You second-guess. You rewind every interaction in your head like a detective at a cold case scene, "Did we say something? Wear the wrong shoes to dinner in 2007?" In this case, we knew it wasn't about us directly. The distance had never been aimed solely at Brittany and me. It had swept through like a storm taking out everyone-our Mom, our Dad, even our favorite aunt and uncle, who were as central to our lives as any immediate relative.

This was still someone we loved but they had become a family we no longer knew. This uncomfortable dilemma hung in the air like stale perfume: Do we just go to the visitation... or do we take off work and attend the funeral, scheduled, inconveniently, right in the middle of the day?

*Of course, you go to the funeral.* That's the right thing to do. Awkwardness and emotional fatigue whispered that *visitation should be enough.*

It was easy to rationalize not going. No one had made an effort to connect. In fact, they had actively ignored the efforts *we* had made to get in touch. Funerals aren't anyone's dream setting for a grand reconnection comeback.

Brittany and I did what sisters do, we processed it to the ground. We floated the idea that I could go for both of us, fulfilling the expectation. We could check the "respectful" box without venturing too far from "emotionally exposed" and "completely inconvenienced" by people who seemingly didn't care about us. Then Brittany had an idea: *Let's call Dad.*

Dad would bring a kind of clear, steady perspective without sugarcoating things. He had once been closest to the person we were grieving. He would undoubtedly carry the heaviest mix of emotion while pretending otherwise. It was also him.

Brittany picked up the phone and filled him in. Do we go? Both of us? Just the visitation? Do you want us there for you?

He didn't hesitate, "Our family has always done the right thing," he said. "This is one of those times."

We knew that. We'd always known that. Sometimes, you ask a question hoping someone will give you permission to take the easier route instead of confirming what you already know to be right.

At the core of the decision, doing the right thing is about identity. It says something about who you are and more importantly, it shapes *who* you become. Doing the right thing, especially when it's uncomfortable, doesn't just reflect your character, it *forms* it.

We went. Just a few quiet acknowledgments, some half-smiles, shallow hugs, and a whole lot of unspoken history swirling around us. We showed up and that mattered.

Life will hand you endless reasons to look the other way or choose ease over effort. Integrity asks more. It asks you to look straight ahead and walk in anyway.

We didn't leave that day with mended fences but we left with peace. The kind that comes from honoring someone's memory and the values that raised us. In a world that often rewards convenience over conscience, choosing to do what's right over what's easy will always set you apart.

# Keep Life in Balance

*"Do you know your Roman numerals?"*

In December of 2024, we gathered at Mom and Dad's house for what had become our little family pre-Christmas gathering with just the immediate crew. It wasn't the full-blown, entire family together holiday extravaganza with casseroles that could feed an army and kids running around all hyped up on cinnamon rolls and Christmas magic. That has shifted to my house now. This one is simpler. Cozier. Just me, Milt, and our daughter Addison, along with Brittany, her husband Matt, and their kids, Caroline and Rhett.

We still met at Mom and Dad's house for this low-key version of the holiday, a tradition we held onto like that one fragile ornament you've had since preschool that makes the tree year after year. The bigger holiday shindigs had long since moved to my house or Brittany's where we had more room. However, this gathering still had its own charm. A cramped living room and the familiar sound of everyone talking over each other to be heard while the little kids ask on repeat, *"When can we open presents?!"* every five minutes.

This year was different. Dad seemed off like he was up to something. He seemed more fidgety than normal.

"Addison, I need you to entertain Caroline and Rhett for a bit. I've got something I need to talk to the mommies and the papas about," Dad said as soon as coats were off and kids were circling the tree like sharks.

This was a curveball.

He was more of a "shout a conversation over frying sausage while the TV's blaring" kind of communicator not one for impromptu "family meetings." For him to call us into a private conversation was off brand.

This definitely wasn't his usual Christmas flair. There were no Walgreens shopping bags filled with an assortment of perfumes, foot scrubs, and "extra manly" body wash. This was something else entirely.

Without explanation, he led us to the back of the house and into what had become Mom's craft room. That space held many identities. It was our childhood playroom, the headquarters for Barbie world domination, and Brittany's bedroom once we declared war on sharing a space during the great Room Divide of '91. It was a room with history, a space that had grown up with us. It felt oddly right that this was where the mystery meeting was going down.

We stood there in that familiar space, glancing around at the walls covered in fabric and yarn, unsure of what was coming. Was this going to be one of those "you'll remember this forever" moments... or just another strange chapter in the ever-expanding Dad files?

"Did y'all study up on your Roman numerals like I told you to?" he asked, starting with a question.

Brittany and I exchanged the universal sister look that translates to, *Oh Lord, we are doing this*. We looked back at him and gave sheepish half-smiles.

About six weeks earlier, Dad had sent us a text one evening that read, "*Do you know Roman numerals?*"

We responded, "A little, why? What are you wanting to know?"

"You should study them."

That was it. No explanation. No follow-up. Just a modern-day scroll from the Oracles of Overalls.

Brittany and I began to dissect the mystery. Maybe he was watching the Super Bowl and got confused about what "LVIII" meant. Maybe it was a late-night Coors Light-fueled brain teaser. Or maybe, and most likely, it was just Dad's way of starting a conversation without the pesky burden of actually *having* one.

Here we were being asked if we'd studied up like we were about to be handed a Scantron test and a No. 2 pencil.

We told him about what we knew, which was pretty basic. Dad just stood there smirk-grinning. He reached into the front pocket of his overalls and pulled out two vacuum-sealed FoodSaver packages. Inside each was a flat rectangle, wrapped in aluminum foil, precisely the length and width of money. He handed one to each of us. On the outside, scrawled in Sharpie, were 2 letters, Roman numerals, with a line over them.

*Our 2024 Christmas gift from Mom and Dad—carefully wrapped in aluminum foil, vacuum-sealed with love.*

"Do you know what that number is?" he asked, in full Dad-Quizmaster mode.

I squinted at mine and piped up. "Yes, I know what these letters represent but you underlined them." "You are looking at it upside down," he said, "the line goes on top of the letters."

Our husbands stood there silently. It was clear they had a pact: *Let the sisters work this out unless it becomes obvious they want help, then offer with extreme caution.*

Dad told us the line on top in Roman Numerals meant the number was multiplied by a thousand. My brain attempted to reboot itself.

One of our husbands finally broke the silence and gently offered, "I think you might be off... by maybe... a zero."

"This is your Christmas gift," he said, matter-of-fact, as if handing over foil-wrapped bundles of cash vacuum-sealed like leftover brisket was the most normal thing in the world.

"Each couple has the same amount," he added, leveling the playing field before anyone could even ask or joke about who his favorite was.

He was also giving us a moment only he could engineer, one that started with a text about Roman numerals and ended with our hands full of vacuum-sealed generosity.

"I wanted to give it to you now because, well, what am I gonna do with it? I don't need it. I would rather *you* have it."

He said it with that signature Dad bluntness, the kind that sounds like a shrug but lands like a gift you didn't know you needed.

Then came the disclaimer.

"Just don't be stupid with it," he warned. "Don't go blow it all in one place. Don't go put it in some college savings account for one of the kids."

We nodded a little stunned, a little teary, and also trying not to laugh because of *course* that's what he thought we would do. Turn it into something responsible.

He continued, "occasionally use it to buy something *fun* or *nice* for yourself. Use it to buy groceries, you know, just normal everyday things like *folding money* is supposed to be used."

He said "folding money" like it was a sacred term. Like it carried an additional value. It was more than money. It was the ability to say yes to something we would normally say no to. It was a reminder not to forget about joy.

It was his way of saying: Live a little. Buy the boots. Take the trip. Splurge on the dessert. Say yes to the thing that makes no practical sense but makes your spirit light up. After all, that is what he did almost every time he walked into Tractor Supply.

The vacuum-sealed mystery had become something else entirely: a nudge, a love letter wrapped in aluminum foil and sealed with intention. It was about what the money *meant*.

Enjoy the now. That was the heart of it. What's the point of working hard, saving smart, and planning carefully, if you never use any of it to actually *live*?

In that cluttered craft room, holding vacuum-sealed envelopes like they were sacred scrolls he was imparting a new lesson: balance. Be practical, yes. Be responsible but also, have a little fun.

On the drive home that night, the car was quiet, Addison half-asleep in the backseat, the glow of holiday lights flickered on either side of the road as Milt steered us through the dark. My mind was racing.

I kept replaying it all. The Roman numeral mystery and the two valuable gifts we received that evening. The meaning behind the gesture and the absurdity and beauty of it all.

Somewhere between Whippoorwill Hill and the Natchez Trace Bridge, I knew I had to write this book.

Not just because the stories are funny (and they are) or because our Dad is unforgettable (which he most definitely is) but because these unconventional life lessons deserve to be named and preserved...for our children and for ourselves. For *anyone* trying to figure out how to live a meaningful *balanced* life in a world that too often pushes us to extremes and overly complicates everything.

We had a front-row seat to a life lived with intention watching how Dad navigated both the ordinary and the extraordinary with Mom as his north star. He wore overalls to birthday parties and dropped coins into beer cans like they were time capsules of wisdom. He didn't say "I love you" in ways you might expect but he made sure you felt it over and over again.

# Afterward

While most of the stories in this book revolve around the unconventional wisdom passed down from Dad, his quotes under chapter titles, teaching without preaching, and his ability to say everything with just a shrug and a metaphor, there's another force woven through every chapter. One who may not always be center stage but whose presence ALWAYS shapes the entire scene: Mom.

Her lessons are more predictable and just as unforgettable. You could see them in what she said and just as powerfully, in what she didn't. You could find them in what she chose to hold together and in what she consciously let go. She taught with trust and by letting us stumble even when every maternal instinct must have been shouting otherwise.

Mom created order in the middle of chaos and embraced the unpredictable without getting lost in it. She is proof that loyalty and strength can exist in the same breath and that being devoted to your family doesn't mean disappearing into the background. She is the ultimate momma bear: fierce when it counts and gentle when it matters most. Rooted in real, authentic relationships, she models what love looks like over the long haul, the day-in, day-out kind that sticks around through the hard parts and finds joy in the ordinary.

She is the balance to Dad's wild card wisdom. The one who keeps things upright while still giving everyone enough room to find their own footing. If Dad taught us how to roll with life's punches, Mom showed us how to stand tall through them. Together, they gave us the full spectrum, humor and grit, comfort and accountability, chaos and calm.

Dad may have gotten most of the lines in these stories, Mom was the foundation they were built on, the reason the stories could unfold the way they did. She was at the heart of it all. Her presence was the thread that tied everything together. Whether she was stepping in with calm certainty or stepping back to let us figure it out, she was always guiding, always shaping. If you look closely, you will see that many of the most meaningful lessons were lived intentionally and with strength.

Together, Mom and Dad built a living example of what real love, marriage, and parenting look like. They showed us marriage was about choosing each other, over and over, especially on the hard days. As parents, they led by consistency and by letting us become ourselves without ever feeling alone in the process. If this book is a collection of life lessons, then they were the ones writing the manual in real time, at different volumes, always together.

# Acknowledgments

To Milt — thank you for giving me the space (and grace) to write. You managed the household and the details while I chased down a memory or wrestled with a paragraph. Thank you for understanding that when I said, *"Just five more minutes,"* what I really meant was *"fifty-five."* Your support made this possible and belief makes me love you even more.

To Brittany Wilder — thank you for being my thinking partner and phone-a-friend while I tried to capture the quirkiness of what we once thought was just a normal life. For someone who gave a definitive "No" to being a co-writer, you somehow still managed to serve as a source of both motivation and encouragement the entire way through. I am lucky to have you!

To Matt Wilder— thank you for being so eager to read this book that it made me nervous it might not meet your expectations. Your enthusiasm held me to a high standard, even as I wrestled with finding the perfect title. I appreciate you searching for the pearls in these pages because we know some people read books "simply because the title sucks them in". Your excitement raised the bar and your feedback arrived at the most critical time.

To Uncle G and Aunt Joyce — there is not a doubt in my mind that I would have hit many more potholes without you. The connections and wisdom you offered made this journey so much more manageable, at a time when shelving this idea for a year (or five) was very tempting. Thank you for allowing me to stand on your shoulders so this manuscript could become something meaningful.

To Mike Reed — I will never look at a "group of three" or a "weasel word" the same way again. Your edits didn't just help make this maiden voyage a reality; they genuinely changed the way I think about writing. I now hear your feedback echoing in my mind every time I sit down to draft ANYTHING. You are a master of your craft, thank you for sharing your talent with me. I better stop there, though... I don't want to give you too much windup and not enough pitch.

To Rick and Pam Burcham — you have been a true blessing. When we first connected, I was ready for the next bite of the elephant and you served me more than I could chew. You believed in me, a girl you barely knew. Thank you for your mentorship and your generous investment of time.

To Tom Carey — *"How's the book coming?"* a question you asked just often enough to keep the fire lit under me. This journey felt daunting before it even began and your faith helped me keep going. I'm grateful for your early read of my manuscript and so sorry you're not here to see it in print but don't worry, I'll make sure Brittany knows you called her Meatball.

To everyone who squealed when you found out I was writing a book and raised a glass to tenacity. Your encouragement came at just the right time. For that, I am deeply grateful. Thank you for believing in the power of a good story — and in mine.

# About the Author

Dr. Alisha Erickson is a lifelong educator and a firm believer in leveraging ordinary moments to teach extraordinary lessons. She holds a Doctorate of Education in Leading Organizations and Strategic Change, along with two master's degrees — one in Educational Leadership and another in Curriculum and  Instruction with an emphasis in Reading. She began her career with a Bachelor of Science in Early Childhood Education and has served as a school principal for more than a decade.

Alisha finds inspiration in the warmth of sunshine and joy in traveling with family and friends. She loves gardening and believes a fresh bouquet of flowers can brighten any space. For her, life's simple luxuries include the crisp feel of fresh linens on a bed, a long hot shower, and the beauty of flower blooms scattered throughout her home. She is rooted in community and energized by people and the stories they carry.

This book is her love letter to the unconventional lessons that shaped her — the ones passed down across kitchen tables and inside cluttered garages. She believes in the value of small gestures and the strength of simply showing up, the kind of grounded wisdom that rarely makes headlines but always makes a difference.

www.ingramcontent.com/pod-product-compliance
Lightning Source LLC
Chambersburg PA
CBHW051626120626
46551CB00014B/1948